Math Engagement
Grade 6

By
M.J. OWEN

COPYRIGHT © 2003 Mark Twain Media, Inc.

ISBN 1-58037-234-1

Printing No. CD-1580

Mark Twain Media, Inc., Publishers
Distributed by Carson-Dellosa Publishing Company, Inc.

Standards reprinted with permission from *Principles and Standards for School Mathematics,* copyright 2000 by the National Council of Teachers of Mathematics. All rights reserved. No endorsement by NCTM is implied.

Table of Contents

Introduction

Based on the National Council of Teachers of Mathematics (NCTM) Standards, this series provides students with multiple grade-appropriate opportunities to practice each skill. Each book contains several practice pages targeting each skill, as well as an assessment page at the end of each section. Periodic reviews of multiple skills are also included throughout the book, in addition to a cumulative assessment. Each assessment and review is set up in standardized-test format.

NCTM STANDARD

Page no.	Number and Operations	Algebra	Geometry	Measurement	Data Analysis, Probability	Problem Solving	Reasoning, Proof	Communication	Connections	Representation
2	x						x			
3	x						x			
4	x				x		x			
5	x						x			
6	x				x		x			
7	x						x			
8	x						x			
9	x									
10	x					x				
11	x									
12	x					x	x			
13	x					x				
14	x					x				
15	x									
16	x					x				
17	x									
18	x					x				
19	x									
20	x						x			
21	x					x				
22	x									
23	x									
24		x			x					
25		x					x			
26		x			x				x	
27		x								
28		x			x					
29		x								
30		x								
31			x			x	x			
32			x				x			
33			x				x			
34			x		x					
35			x				x			
36			x				x			
37			x							
38			x		x					
39			x							
40		x	x							
41		x	x							
42	x	x	x							
43		x	x							

NCTM STANDARD

Page no.	Number and Operations	Algebra	Geometry	Measurement	Data Analysis, Probability	Problem Solving	Reasoning, Proof	Communication	Connections	Representation
44		x					x			
45		x					x			
46		x				x				
47		x					x			
48		x					x			
49		x					x			
50		x					x			x
51		x								
52		x								x
53	x	x								
54	x	x								
55		x					x			
56			x					x		
57			x							
58			x							
59			x							
60			x				x			
61	x		x							
62	x		x			x				
63	x	x	x			x				
64	x	x	x							
65	x	x	x							
66	x	x					x			
67	x	x								
68					x					
69					x			x	x	x
70					x					
71					x		x			
72					x		x			
73					x		x			
74					x	x	x			
75					x				x	
76					x					x
77					x		x			
78					x					
79					x		x			
80					x	x	x			
81					x		x	x		
82					x					
83		·			x					
84	x		x	x	x	x				

Name: _____ Date: _____

Skill: Understanding numbers, the ways of representing numbers, relationships among numbers, and number systems

Unit 1: Number and Operations: *Practice Activity 1*

Did you know that there are many ways to write the same number? Try writing each of the following numbers in three different forms: word form, standard form, and expanded form. Look at the example before you get started.

> *Example:* 15,987,978
> **word form:** fifteen million, nine hundred eighty-seven thousand, nine hundred seventy-eight
> **standard form:** 15,987,978
> **expanded form:** 10,000,000 + 5,000,000 + 900,000 + 80,000 + 7,000 + 900 + 70 + 8

1. 87,989,009

   word form: _____

   standard form: _____

   expanded form: _____

2. 12,897,098

   word form: _____

   standard form: _____

   expanded form: _____

3. 309,897

   word form: _____

   standard form: _____

   expanded form: _____

4. 67,098,981

   word form: _____

   standard form: _____

   expanded form: _____

5. 21,987,767

   word form: _____

   standard form: _____

   expanded form: _____

Name: _____ Date: _____

Unit 1: Number and Operations: *Practice Activity 1 (cont.)*

6. 809,987

word form: _____

standard form: _____

expanded form: _____

7. 10,989,543

word form: _____

standard form: _____

expanded form: _____

8. 65,987,877

word form: _____

standard form: _____

expanded form: _____

9. 2,098,871

word form: _____

standard form: _____

expanded form: _____

10. 98,786,111

word form: _____

standard form: _____

expanded form: _____

Name: _____   Date: _____

Skill: Understanding numbers, ways of representing numbers, relationships among numbers, and number systems

Unit 1: Number and Operations: *Practice Activity 2*

Just a Tip: The value of a number depends on the place that it holds. Try making a place value chart for each number to help you determine each number's value.

Read each number. Write the value of the number in bold on the line.

Example:

6	7	8	0	9	8	2	3	5
Millions	Hundred-Thousands	Ten-Thousands	Thousands	Hundreds	Tens	Ones	Tenths	Hundredths	Thousandths

Answer: 70,000

1. 45,876,00**5** _____

2. **9**0,987,876 _____

3. 80**5**,876,321,098 _____

4. **9**87,765,444,001 _____

5. 79,098,7**6**5 _____

6. **3**80,987,765,555 _____

7. 765,88**8** _____

8. **2**.987 _____

9. 0.00**5** _____

10. **1**3,212,898 _____

11. 787,9**9**0,001 _____

12. 6.3**2**8 _____

13. 17.9**0**8 _____

14. 0.1**3** _____

15. 68,**9**87,003 _____

WAKE-UP WORD PROBLEM: Two hundred forty students from Deguire Middle School are going on a field trip. Seventy-five percent of the students brought a sack lunch from home. The rest of the students ordered a lunch from the cafeteria. How many students bought a lunch from the cafeteria?

Name: _____ Date: _____

Skill: Understanding numbers, ways of representing numbers, relationships among numbers, and number systems

Unit 1: Number and Operations: *Practice Activity 3*

Look at each of the models below. Determine how much of each model is shaded. Write the amount of each model shaded as a fraction, decimal, percent, and ratio.

Example:

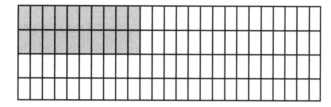

Fraction: $\frac{1}{5}$ **Decimal:** 0.20   **Percent:** 20%   **Ratio:** 20:100

1. Fraction: _____
    Decimal: _____
    Percent: _____
    Ratio: _____

2. Fraction: _____
    Decimal: _____
    Percent: _____
    Ratio: _____

3. Fraction: _____
    Decimal: _____
    Percent: _____
    Ratio: _____

4. Fraction: _____
    Decimal: _____
    Percent: _____
    Ratio: _____

5. Fraction: _____
    Decimal: _____
    Percent: _____
    Ratio: _____

Name: _____ Date: _____

Unit 1: Number and Operations: *Practice Activity 3 (cont.)*

6. Fraction: _____

     Decimal: _____

     Percent: _____

     Ratio: _____

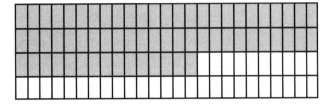

7. Fraction: _____

     Decimal: _____

     Percent: _____

     Ratio: _____

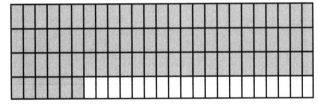

8. Fraction: _____

     Decimal: _____

     Percent: _____

     Ratio: _____

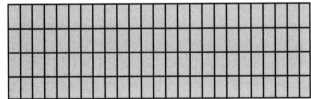

9. Fraction: _____

     Decimal: _____

     Percent: _____

     Ratio: _____

Write each fraction, decimal, or ratio as a percent.

Example: $\frac{1}{100}$; 0.01; 1:100 = 1%

10. 25:100 _____

11. $\frac{17}{100}$ _____

12. 0.75 _____

13. 0.84 _____

14. 2:100 _____

WAKE-UP WORD PROBLEM: Three hundred fifty kids are signed up for summer camp. Fifty percent of the students that are signed up for camp are boys. The rest of the campers are girls. How many girls are signed up to attend summer camp?

Name: _____ Date: _____

Skill: Understanding numbers, ways of representing numbers, relationships among numbers, and number systems

Unit 1: Number and Operations: *Practice Activity 4*

Circle the larger fraction and/or decimal.

    Example: $\frac{5}{6}$ $\frac{7}{8}$ *Answer:* $\frac{7}{8}$

Just a Tip: If you are having trouble determining the larger number, try converting each fraction and/or decimal to a percent, ratio, and/or decimal. Then compare the numbers again.

1.   0.001   0.0001

2. $\frac{1}{4}$ $\frac{2}{9}$

3.   0.234   0.301

4.   5.05   5.55

Put each set of numbers in order from greatest to least.

5.   9,098,987; 19,878,098; 9,008,098; 9,876,098

    _____

6.   210,098,876; 211,098,876; 210,876,098; 210,546,876

    _____

7.   6,987,987; 3,546,876; 6,987,098; 6,432,098

    _____

8.   788,654; 786,876; 708,876; 788,091; 788,543

    _____

9.   21,098,876; 21,765,908; 21,987,096; 21,543,765

    _____

Put each set of decimals in order from least to greatest.

10.   0.001; 0.01; 1.0; 0.0001 _____

11.   0.78; 0.87; 0.007; 0.70 _____

12.   0.67; 0.06; 0.076; 0.0072 _____

13.   0.34; 0.42; 0.043; 0.074 _____

14.   0.210; 2.10; 0.0210; 0.0021 _____

Name: _____ Date: _____

Skill: Understanding numbers, ways of representing numbers, relationships among numbers, and number systems

Unit 1: Number and Operations: *Assessment 1*

Read each question carefully. Then mark the best answer.

1. Which answer represents the number 876,098,543 written in word form?
   - ○ A. eight hundred seventy-six million, ninety-eight thousand, five hundred fourteen
   - ○ B. eight-hundred seventy-six million, ninety-eight thousand, five hundred forty-three
   - ○ C. eight hundred seventy-six billion, ninety-eight thousand, five hundred forty-three
   - ○ D. eight hundred seventy-six million, ninety-eight hundred, five hundred forty-three

2. What is the value of the number in bold?
   876,**9**08,001
   - ○ A. 700,000,000
   - ○ B. 70,000,000
   - ○ C. 7,000,000
   - ○ D. 76,000,000

3. Which fraction represents the decimal 0.007?
   - ○ A. $\frac{7}{100}$
   - ○ B. $\frac{7}{10}$
   - ○ C. $\frac{7}{1000}$
   - ○ D. $\frac{70}{100}$

4. Which percentage represents the fraction $\frac{9}{10}$?
   - ○ A. 9%
   - ○ B. 19%
   - ○ C. 90%
   - ○ D. 900%

5. Which percentage represents the fraction $\frac{9}{100}$?
   - ○ A. 9%
   - ○ B. 19%
   - ○ C. 90%
   - ○ D. 900%

6. Which decimal represents the part of the model that is shaded?
   - ○ A. 17.07
   - ○ B. 0.17
   - ○ C. 0.017
   - ○ D. 0.070

   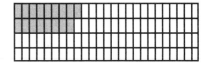

7. Which fraction represents the part of the model that is not shaded?
   - ○ A. $\frac{75}{100}$
   - ○ B. $\frac{76}{100}$
   - ○ C. $\frac{24}{100}$
   - ○ D. $\frac{25}{100}$

   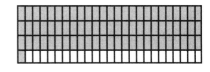

8. What is the value of the number in bold?
   2**0**9,098,098
   - ○ A. 20,000,000
   - ○ B. 2,000,000
   - ○ C. 209,000,000
   - ○ D. 200,000,000

Name: _____   Date: _____

Unit 1: Number and Operations: *Assessment 1 (cont.)*

9. Which of the following shows the number 43,984,899 in expanded form?
    - ○ A. 40,000,000 + 3,000,000 + 900,000 + 80,000 + 4,000 + 800 + 90 + 9
    - ○ B. 40,000 + 3,000,000 + 900,000 + 80,000 + 4,000 + 800 + 99
    - ○ C. 40,000,000 + 30,000,000 + 900,000 + 80,000 + 4,000 + 800 + 90 + 9
    - ○ D. 40,000,000 + 3,000,000 + 90,000 + 80,000 + 4,000 + 800 + 90 + 9

10. Which of the following represents the number 9,897,878 in expanded form?
    - ○ A. 9,000,000 + 90,000 + 800,000 + 7,000 + 800 + 70 + 8
    - ○ B. 900,000 + 80,000 + 90,000 + 7,000 + 800 + 70 + 8
    - ○ C. 9,000,000 + 800,000 + 900 + 700 + 800 + 70 + 8
    - ○ D. 9,000,000 + 800,000 + 90,000 + 7,000 + 800 + 70 + 8

11. Which of the following shows the numbers in order from greatest to least?
    - ○ A. 432,321,987; 432,897,098; 433,987,654; 423,967,091
    - ○ B. 423,967,091; 432,321,987; 432,897,098; 433,987,654
    - ○ C. 433,987,654; 432,897,098; 432,321,987; 423,967,091
    - ○ D. 433,987,654; 432,897,098; 423,967,091; 432,321,987

12. Which of the following has the smallest value?
    - ○ A. 0.004
    - ○ B. 0.75
    - ○ C. 0.075
    - ○ D. 0.079

13. Which percentage represents the decimal 0.78?
    - ○ A. 78%
    - ○ B. 87%
    - ○ C. 780%
    - ○ D. 7%

14. Which of the following lists the decimals in order from least to greatest?
    - ○ A. 0.987; 0.897; 0.098; 0.088
    - ○ B. 0.088; 0.098; 0.897; 0.987
    - ○ C. 0.088; 0.098; 0.987; 0.897
    - ○ D. 0.987; 0.098; 0.897; 0.088

15. Which of the following is equivalent to the fraction $\frac{8}{10}$?
    - ○ A. 8%
    - ○ B. 80%
    - ○ C. 18%
    - ○ D. 800%

Name: _____   Date: _____

Skill: Understanding the meanings of operations and how they relate to each other

Unit 1: Number and Operations: *Practice Activity 5*

Please solve the following fifteen problems. You may use your calculator to solve these problems.

> ***Example:*** 0.089 x 0.076 ÷ 2.23 = 0.003033183

1. 96 x 189 ÷ 86 = _____

2. 0.114 x 0.32 ÷ 5 = _____

3. 1.43 x 6.54 ÷ 4 = _____

4. 4,543 x 2,321 ÷ 2 = _____

5. 50 x 0.005 ÷ 10 = _____

6. 908 x 432 ÷ 0.24 = _____

7. 1,621 x 345 ÷ 0.08 = _____

8. 1,356 x 654 ÷ 0.02 = _____

9. 174 x 189 ÷ 12 = _____

10. 2,344 x 133 ÷ 6 = _____

11. 2,500,000 x 2 ÷ 50 = _____

12. 789 x 0.009 ÷ 0.6 = _____

13. 4,323 x 903 ÷ 4 = _____

14. 285 x 314 ÷ 24 x 8 = _____

WAKE-UP WORD PROBLEM: Mark works at the grocery store after school. He earns $424.79 each month. How much money does Mark earn in one year?

_____

Name: _____ Date: _____

Skill: Understanding the meanings of operations and how they relate to each other

Unit 1: Number and Operations: *Practice Activity 6*

Read each word problem. On the first line, write the number sentence that should be used to solve the problem. Then, write the solution on the second line. Some of these problems may be two-step problems. Some of these problems may have remainders. Students may use their own scrap paper if needed.

Just a Tip: Practice working two-step problems with students. Have students practice reading the problem once or twice. Then ask, "What are you looking for?" Have students write a sentence that leaves out the answer but tells what they are looking for. (*For example:* Students read the problem: "Mary has $0.79. She spends $0.21 on two jawbreakers. On the way home, Mary finds a quarter. How much money does Mary have now?" Ask students what they are looking for. Then have them form an answer sentence that reminds them of the information they are looking for and how to solve the problem, "Mary has _____ money now." First you need to find out how much she spent: $0.79 - $0.21 = $0.58. Then you add the money she found: $0.58 + $0.25 = $0.83.)

1. Three brothers work during the month of July. Rick earns $216.75, Chris earns $14.75 less than Rick, and Tom earns $78.95 more than Chris. How much money does Tom earn during the month of July?

    _____

    _____

2. Sarah Lee is collecting money for charity. She collects $289.50 during a ten-day period. She collects about the same amount of money each day. About how much money does Sarah Lee collect each day?

    _____

    _____

3. The Police Department responds to 182 emergency calls during November. They respond to twice as many emergency calls during December and one-half as many calls during January as they did in December. How many calls does the Police Department respond to during January?

    _____

    _____

4. Denise buys one hundred eighty-six bags of hamburger buns for the school picnic. There are twenty-four hamburger buns in each bag. How many hamburger buns does Denise buy in all?

    _____

    _____

Name: _____ Date: _____

Unit 1: Number and Operations: *Practice Activity 6 (cont.)*

5. Laurel is comparing prices on bottled water. At her neighborhood grocery store, she can purchase twelve bottles of water for $5.00. At a large discount store, she can purchase twenty-four bottles for $6.99. About how much less per bottle will it cost Laurel to buy bottled water at the discount store?

    _____

    _____

6. Mr. Craig spends $85.50 on his electricity bill during March. He spends three times as much on his electricity during the month of June. How much money does Mr. Craig spend on his electricity bill during June?

    _____

    _____

7. James wants to save 0.10, or 10%, of the money he earns during June, July, and August to help him pay for things he might need during the school year. He earns $430.00 during each month during the summer working as a lifeguard. How much money will James be able to save?

    _____

    _____

8. Stella wants to figure out the number of minutes in one year. She knows that there are sixty minutes in one hour and twenty-four hours in one day. How many minutes are in one year?

    _____

    _____

9. Pedro, Lupe, and Mario all have large marble collections. Pedro has 514 marbles in his collection. Lupe has 212 fewer marbles than Pedro, and Mario has 216 more marbles than Lupe. How many marbles does Mario have in his collection?

    _____

    _____

Extension Activity: Give each student ten index cards. Have students write five two-step problems on five of their index cards. Then, direct students to write five "answer sentences" on the remaining five index cards. Now, have students switch cards with a classmate. Ask students to match two-step problems with the correct answer sentences. This could also be done with partners or as group work.

Name: _____ Date: _____

Skill: Understanding the meanings of operations and how they relate to each other

Unit 1: Number and Operations: *Practice Activity 7*

Look at each example. Write a number sentence next to the sentence given that shows an example of each property.

Just a Tip: When you multiply two integers, first multiply the numbers without their signs. Remember that when two integers have the same signs, the product will be positive. When two integers have different signs, the product will be negative.

Commutative Property of Multiplication (Integers):
    Example: -3 x 4 = 4 x -3 =

1. -6 x 2 = _____   **2.** 5 x -3 = _____

Associative Property of Multiplication (Integers):
    Example: (-3 x 4) x -2 = -3 x (4 x -2)

3. (-2 x 4) x -3 = _____   **4.** 2 x (3 x -2) = _____

Identity Property of Multiplication (Integers):
    Example: -3 x 1 = -3

5. -5 x 1 = _____   **6.** 1 x -6 = _____

Zero Property of Multiplication (Integers):
    Example: -3 x 0 = 0

7. -2 x 0 = _____   **8.** 0 x -7 = _____

Distributive Property of Multiplication over Addition (Integers):
    Example: -3 x (4 + -2) = (-3 x 4) + (-3 x -2)

9. -2 x (3 + -4) = _____   **10.** -3 x (5 + 6) = _____

Distributive Property of Multiplication over Subtraction (Integers):
    Example: -3 x (4 - -2) = (-3 x 4) - (-3 x -2)

11. -4 x (2 - 5) = _____   **12.** -6 x (3 - 6) = _____

Solve these problems.

13. -3 x 6 = _____   **14.** -4 x -5 = _____

15. -2 x -6 = _____

WAKE-UP WORD PROBLEM: The temperature on Saturday is 85° Fahrenheit. During the week, the temperature drops two degrees every day. By the following Friday, what is the temperature?

_____

Name: _____   Date: _____

Skill: Understanding the meanings of operations and how they relate to each other

Unit 1: Number and Operations: *Assessment 2*

Mark the best answer for the following problems.

1. $145 \div 4 \times 0.95 =$
    - ○ A. 3443.75
    - ○ B. 34.4375
    - ○ C. 36.25
    - ○ D. 36.75

2. $11 \times -5 =$
    - ○ A. 50
    - ○ B. 55
    - ○ C. -50
    - ○ D. -55

Mark the answer that shows the correct number sentence to solve the problem.

3. Jake and Dana spend a total of $112.95 when they are on vacation. Assuming each child spends approximately the same amount of money, how much money does each spend?
    - ○ A. $112.95 x 2 = $225.90
    - ○ B. $112.95 ÷ 5 = $22.59
    - ○ C. $112.95 ÷ 2 = $56.475
    - ○ D. $112.95 x 3 = $338.85

4. Seventeen people work at the movie theater over the weekend. Each employee earns $7.75 per hour. Over the weekend, each employee works twelve hours. How much money do all seventeen employees earn altogether?
    - ○ A. 17 x $7.75 ÷ 12 = $10.979
    - ○ B. 17 + $7.75 x 12 = $297.00
    - ○ C. $7.75 x 12 x 17 = $1,581.00
    - ○ D. $7.75 ÷ 17 x 12 = $5.47

5. The temperature on Wednesday is 92° Fahrenheit. During an unusual cold front, the temperature drops 3 degrees every day. What is the temperature the following Wednesday?
    - ○ A. 92° - 3 = 89°F
    - ○ B. 92° + (3 x 7) = 113°F
    - ○ C. (92° - 3) x 7 = 623°F
    - ○ D. 92° - (3 x 7) = 71°F

Name: _____ Date: _____

Unit 1: Number and Operations: *Assessment 2 (cont.)*

Identify the property used in each example.

6. -5 x 0 =
- ○ A. Commutative Property of Multiplication
- ○ B. Identity Property of Multiplication
- ○ C. Zero Property of Multiplication
- ○ D. Distributive Property of Multiplication over Subtraction

7. (-5 x 2) x -3 = -5 x (2 x -3)
- ○ A. Commutative Property of Multiplication
- ○ B. Associative Property of Multiplication
- ○ C. Identity Property of Multiplication
- ○ D. Zero Property of Multiplication

8. -3 x (4 - -6) = (-3 x 4) - (-3 x -6)
- ○ A. Associative Property of Multiplication
- ○ B. Commutative Property of Multiplication
- ○ C. Distributive Property of Multiplication over Subtraction
- ○ D. Distributive Property of Multiplication over Addition

Multiply.

9. -8 x -8 =
- ○ A. 60
- ○ B. 64
- ○ C. -64
- ○ D. -16

10. 5 x -7 =
- ○ A. -35
- ○ B. 35
- ○ C. -32
- ○ D. -12

11. -9 x 6 =
- ○ A. 54
- ○ B. -52
- ○ C. -54
- ○ D. 56

12. -7 x -8 =
- ○ A. 56
- ○ B. -56
- ○ C. -54
- ○ D. 54

Name: _____ Date: _____

Skill: Computing fluently and making reasonable estimates

Unit 1: Number and Operations: *Practice Activity 8*

Just a Tip: Round each number and/or decimal to the thousands place before adding or subtracting.

Estimate each sum or difference to the nearest thousand. The first one has been completed as an example.

Example:

1. 40,089 - 23,987 = _(Think: 40,000 - 24,000 = 16,000)_

2. 31,578 - 17,865 = _____

3. 165,657 - 123,342 = _____

4. 88,786 - 33,453 = _____

5. 234,311 - 45,765 = _____

6. 33,765 + 81,098 = _____

7. 19,987 - 2,343 = _____

8. 21,234 + 65,765 = _____

9. 88,987 - 34,543 = _____

10. 10,987 + 13,453 = _____

11. 23,432 - 4,433 = _____

12. 675,432 - 34,454 = _____

WAKE-UP WORD PROBLEM: About seven hundred eighty-nine people attended a concert on Friday night. On Saturday night, about nine hundred eleven people attended the same concert. About how many people attended the concert on both Friday and Saturday nights?

_____

Name: _____　Date: _____

Skill: Computing fluently and making reasonable estimates

Unit 1: Number and Operations: *Practice Activity 9*

Round each number to the nearest hundred thousand. ***Example:*** 543,232　*Answer:* 500,000

1. 1,234,432 _____

2. 987,777 _____

3. 434,232 _____

4. 2,343,123 _____

5. 1,992,075 _____

Round each number to the nearest million. ***Example:*** 73,934,507　*Answer:* 74,000,000

6. 7,987,878 _____

7. 12,123,121 _____

8. 9,098,987 _____

9. 1,002,323 _____

10. 2,332,334 _____

Round each number to the nearest tenth. ***Example:*** $12.75　*Answer:* $12.80

11. $34.23 _____

12. $234.43 _____

13. $12.343 _____

14. $45.765 _____

15. $35.43 _____

Round each number to the nearest hundredth. ***Example:*** $652.084　*Answer:* $652.08

16. $122.892 _____

17. $1,232.985 _____

18. $676.507 _____

19. $432.444 _____

20. $1,088.356 _____

Extension Activity: Have students cut out and read two to three articles from the newspaper that include numbers. Instruct them to highlight each number in the article. Then have them round each number.

Name: _____ Date: _____

Skill: Computing fluently and making reasonable estimates

Unit 1: Number and Operations: *Practice Activity 10*

Read each word problem. First, round each number. Then, determine the best estimate of the answer. Finally, write a complete sentence that gives the answer to the word problem.

Example: Mary spends $513.75 on groceries during the month of January. During the month of February, she spends $395.79. About how much more money did Mary spend on groceries during the month of January than in February?

$500.00 - $400.00 = $100.00

Mary spent about $100.00 more on groceries during the month of January.

1. Caroline works 27.5 hours per week. Her brother, Craig, works 18.5 hours per week. About how many hours do Caroline and Craig work altogether?

2. Smithville has a population of 1,321,675. Jonestown has a population of 21,987. About how many people live in Smithville and Jonestown combined?

3. Hannah has just signed up to play soccer. She spends $95.75 registering for the season, $45.95 on a new pair of cleats, and $38.75 purchasing a uniform. About how much money does Hannah spend on all three items combined?

4. Mr. Wilson is spending $104,675 renovating his home. His next-door neighbor, Mr. Perez, is spending $58,998 renovating his home. About how much more money will Mr. Wilson spend renovating his home than Mr. Perez?

Name: _____   Date: _____

Unit 1: Number and Operations: *Practice Activity 10 (cont.)*

5. Maggie earns money babysitting for four consecutive Saturday nights. She earns $23.45 the first Saturday night, $25.50 the second Saturday night, $31.95 the third Saturday night, and $18.75 the fourth Saturday night. About how much money does Maggie earn babysitting for four consecutive Saturday nights?

_____

_____

6. Three friends count the amount of change they have in their front pockets. Li has $0.89, Patrice has $0.41, and Roseanne has $0.55. About how much money do Li, Patrice, and Roseanne have altogether?

_____

_____

7. Mary Katherine wants to order a game online. She investigates two websites, looking for the best price. She finds the game priced at $43.95 on the first website and $56.50 on the second. About how much money can Mary Katherine save if she buys the game at the first website?

_____

_____

Name: _____ Date: _____

Skill: Computing fluently and making reasonable estimates

Unit 1: Number and Operations: *Assessment 3*

Follow the directions above each problem. Then mark the best answer to the problem.

Round each number to the nearest hundred thousand.

1. 345,123
   - ○ A. 250,000
   - ○ B. 300,000
   - ○ C. 350,000
   - ○ D. 400,000

2. 2,473,122
   - ○ A. 2,480,000
   - ○ B. 2,470,000
   - ○ C. 2,400,000
   - ○ D. 2,500,000

Round each number to the nearest million.

3. 5,231,212
   - ○ A. 5,230,000
   - ○ B. 5,200,000
   - ○ C. 6,000,000
   - ○ D. 5,000,000

4. 13,232,123
   - ○ A. 13,000,000
   - ○ B. 13,200,000
   - ○ C. 14,000,000
   - ○ D. 12,000,000

Round each number to the nearest hundredth.

5. $78.985
   - ○ A. $78.99
   - ○ B. $78.75
   - ○ C. $80.00
   - ○ D. $79.75

6. $85.900
   - ○ A. $85.95
   - ○ B. $85.90
   - ○ C. $85.00
   - ○ D. $90.00

Round each number to the nearest tenth.

7. 0.897
   - ○ A. 0.889
   - ○ B. 0.900
   - ○ C. 0.9
   - ○ D. 0.10

8. $32.987
   - ○ A. $33.90
   - ○ B. $33.00
   - ○ C. $32.99
   - ○ D. $35.00

Name: _____ Date: _____

Unit 1: Number and Operations: *Assessment 3 (cont.)*

Estimate the sum or difference for each problem by rounding to the nearest thousand before computing.

9. 17,675 - 3,432 =
   - ○ A. 12,000
   - ○ B. 15,000
   - ○ C. 14,000
   - ○ D. 15,000

10. 167,987 - 112,002 =
    - ○ A. 300,000
    - ○ B. 55,500
    - ○ C. 56,000
    - ○ D. 58,000

Solve each word problem, and then round to get the answer.

11. Carrie is having a birthday party. She spends $21.55 on invitations, $35.95 on decorations, and $45.79 on lunch. About how much money did Carrie spend in all on her birthday party?
    - ○ A. $103.00
    - ○ B. $104.00
    - ○ C. $114.00
    - ○ D. $112.50

12. Ms. Garcia and Mr. Woods both teach school. Ms. Garcia earns $32,987.00 a year. Mr. Woods earns $33,765 a year. About how much money do Ms. Garcia and Mr. Woods earn altogether?
    - ○ A. $64,900
    - ○ B. $67,500
    - ○ C. $68,000
    - ○ D. $67,000

Name: _____ Date: _____

Review of Three Previously Taught NCTM Standards

- **Understanding numbers, ways of representing numbers, relationships among numbers, and number systems**

- **Understanding the meanings of operations and how they relate to each other**

- **Computing fluently and making reasonable estimates**

1. Round the number to the nearest tenth: $15.65
   - ○ A. $15.7
   - ○ B. $15.8
   - ○ C. $16.00
   - ○ D. $15.9

2. Round the number to the nearest million: 12,876,987
   - ○ A. 12,000,000
   - ○ B. 12,850,000
   - ○ C. 13,000,000
   - ○ D. 12,870,000

3. Which of the following represents the number 543,273 in expanded form?
   - ○ A. 5,000,000 + 400,000 + 30,000 + 2,000 + 700 + 3
   - ○ B. 500,000 + 40,000 + 30,000 + 200 + 70 + 3
   - ○ C. 500,000 + 40,000 + 3,000 + 200 + 70 + 3
   - ○ D. 500,000 + 45,000 + 3,000 + 200 + 70 + 3

4. Which of the following represents the number seven million, eight hundred forty-eight thousand, six hundred fifteen in number form?
   - ○ A. 7,848,065
   - ○ B. 784,861
   - ○ C. 7,848,651
   - ○ D. 7,848,615

5. Which model represents the decimal 0.75?

   ○ A.    ○ C.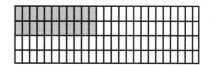

   ○ B.    ○ D.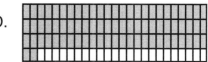

Name: _____ Date: _____

Review of Three Previously Taught NCTM Standards (cont.)

6. Which of the following shows the numbers in order from least to greatest?
   ○ A. 34,543; 35,503; 34,675; 35,992; 36,001
   ○ B. 36,001; 35,992; 35,503; 34,675; 34,543
   ○ C. 35,543; 34,675; 35,992; 35,503; 36,001
   ○ D. 34,543; 34,675; 35,503; 35,992; 36,001

7. Solve the problem: 2,487 x 6 ÷ 3 =
   ○ A. 9,744
   ○ B. 4,904
   ○ C. 4,971
   ○ D. 4,974

8. Which of the following properties is this equation an example of?
   (-4 x 3) x -2 = -4 x (3 x -2)
   ○ A. Commutative Property
   ○ B. Identity Property
   ○ C. Associative Property
   ○ D. Zero Property

Round each sum and/or difference to the nearest thousand.

9. 127,876 - 34,765 =
   ○ A. 163,000
   ○ B. 98,000
   ○ C. 93,000
   ○ D. 95,000

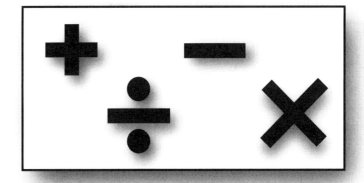

10. 233,765 + 113,000 =
   ○ A. 347,000
   ○ B. 348,000
   ○ C. 347,500
   ○ D. 387,098

11. Which percent represents the ratio 17:100?
   ○ A. 21%
   ○ B. 71%
   ○ C. 17%
   ○ D. 170%

12. Solve the problem: 4 x 20 ÷ 10 =
   ○ A. 6
   ○ B. 8
   ○ C. 4
   ○ D. 10

Name: _____   Date: _____

Skill: Understanding patterns, relations, and functions

Unit 2: Algebra: *Practice Activity 1*

Complete the following numeric patterns.

Example: 115, 104, _____, _____, 71, 60 *Answer:* 115, 104, 93, 82, 71, 60
                                                              -11 -11 -11 -11 -11 -11

1. 9, 27, _____, 243, _____, 2,187

2. 1,856, 928, _____, _____, 116

3. 801, 817, _____, _____, 865, 881

4. 17, 51, 204, 612, _____, _____, 29,376, 88,128

Complete the table for each function.

Just a Tip: A function is a relationship in which one quantity depends on another quantity. Let *w* represent the weight in pounds. Let *c* represent the cost of shipping the package.

Maria is ordering merchandise from the "Stickers and More" catalog. Stickers, albums, and album pages are all available. The cost of shipping merchandise is $3.00, plus $0.95 per pound.

Look at the table, and then answer each question.

Weight in pounds:	1	2	3	4	5
Shipping cost in dollars:	$3.95			$6.80	

5. How much shipping will Maria pay if her order weighs two pounds? _____

6. How much shipping will Maria pay if her order weighs three pounds? _____

7. How much shipping will Maria pay if her order weighs five pounds? _____

8. Write the equation that you used to figure out the cost of shipping five pounds worth of merchandise. _____

9. Maria will pay $6.80 if her package weighs _____ pounds.

WAKE-UP WORD PROBLEM: Mika orders $78.95 in merchandise from her favorite catalog. She has to pay $6.32 tax on the merchandise and $15.75 for shipping and handling charges. How much will Mika's shipment cost her in all?

_____

Name: _____ Date: _____

Skill: Understanding patterns, relations, and functions

Unit 2: Algebra: *Practice Activity 2*

Tasha visits the website of her favorite rock band. She wants to purchase a poster of the band, which is available in several sizes. No matter which size Tasha decides to purchase, the width for every poster is 5 inches more than twice its length.

Look at the table. Then answer each question.

Length in inches	6	10	12	
Width in inches		25		35

1. If the poster is six inches in length, what will the width be? _____

2. If the length is twelve inches, what will the width be? _____

3. If the width is thirty-five inches, what will the length be? _____

Complete the following numeric patterns.

4. 4.5, 9.9, _____, _____, 105.4, _____

5. 396, 1,584, 6,336, _____, _____, _____

6. 2,015, 2,008, _____, _____, _____, 1,980

Look at the table. Then answer questions 7–9.

Pattern #	2	4	6	8
Picture	***	*** ***		****** ******
# of stars	3	6	9	

7. What should the picture look like for pattern #6? _____

8. How many stars should go with pattern #8? _____

9. Which equation could represent the function of the graph? _____

Name: _____   Date: _____

Skill: Understanding patterns, relations, and functions

Unit 2: Algebra: *Assessment 1*

Fill in the missing numbers in each pattern.

1. 17, 68, 340, 1,360, 6,800, _____, _____, _____

2. 12,545, 12,536, _____, _____, 12,509, _____

3. 1,028, 514, _____, _____, 64.25, _____

4. 7, 63, _____, 5,103, 45,927

5. 789, 778, 766, _____, 739, _____

Look at the table. Then answer questions 6–10.

James just ordered some new shirts to wear when he goes back to school. The cost of shipping for the shirts is $5.00 plus $0.75 per pound.

Weight in pounds:	1	3	5	7	9	11
Shipping cost in dollars:		$6.50		$8.00		

6. How much would James spend on shipping if his item(s) weighs one pound? _____

7. How much would James spend on shipping if his item(s) weighs five pounds? _____

8. How much would James spend on shipping if his item(s) weighs eleven pounds? _____

9. James spends $11.75 on shipping. How much do his items weigh? _____

10. What equation could be used to determine the function of this table? _____

_____

Extension Activity: Find something in your everyday life that you could put on a function table, and then create one. Share it with your classmates.

Name: _____ Date: _____

Skill: Representing and analyzing mathematical situations and structures using algebraic symbols

Unit 2: Algebra: *Practice Activity 3*

Evaluate each expression and find the number that is represented by the variable.

Example: $7.2 \times y = 108$ $y = 15$

1. $126.4 \div x = 31.6$ $x =$ _____

2. $18.4 \times r = 496.8$ $r =$ _____

3. $458.2 \div c = 57.275$ $c =$ _____

4. $32.2 \times b = 1674.4$ $b =$ _____

5. $99 \div t = 33$ $t =$ _____

6. $12.9 \times q = 219.3$ $q =$ _____

7. $658.35 \div m = 73.15$ $m =$ _____

8. $675 \times p = 23,625$ $p =$ _____

9. $67.4 \times u = 1,213.2$ $u =$ _____

10. $256 \times d = 24,320$ $d =$ _____

11. $54.67 \div a = 7.81$ $a =$ _____

12. $79.4 \times z = 873.4$ $z =$ _____

13. $915.6 \div n = 30.52$ $n =$ _____

14. $2.079 \times s = 324.324$ $s =$ _____

15. $7,122.5 \div v = 284.9$ $v =$ _____

Name: _____ Date: _____

Skill: Representing and analyzing mathematical situations and structure using algebraic symbols

Unit 2: Algebra: *Practice Activity 4*

Solve each equation. Try to get the variable alone on one side of the equation.

Example: $25n + 9 = 84$; $25n + 9 - 9 = 84 - 9$; $25n \div 25 = 75 \div 25$; $n = 3$

1. $8x + 8 = 24$ $x =$ _____

2. $\frac{d}{8} + 21 = 27$ $d =$ _____

3. $\frac{y}{5} + 18 = 25$ $y =$ _____

4. $1.9r \times 14 = 159.6$ $r =$ _____

5. $18z \times 3 = 216$ $z =$ _____

6. $8x + 34 = 98$ $x =$ _____

7. $\frac{1}{2}h + \frac{3}{4} = 4\frac{3}{4}$ $h =$ _____

8. $17t - 11 = 176$ $t =$ _____

9. $21u - 9 = 306$ $u =$ _____

10. $37r - 23 = 458$ $r =$ _____

Complete the table. Use the values given for each variable to solve for the other variable.

	Rule: $y = 0.79 + 4.3(x)$	
	x	**y**
11.	2	
12.	3.7	
13.		18.85
14.	4.6	
15.	5.2	

Just a Tip: Solve the problem below by setting up an equation. Select a letter to represent each variable.

WAKE-UP WORD PROBLEM: Quinn's mom is hosting a large formal party. She needs to rent twenty-five tables and three hundred chairs for her gathering. It costs $10 to rent each table and $28.75 to rent a set of fifty chairs. How much will it cost Quinn's mom to rent all of the tables and chairs she needs for the party?

_____

Name: _____ Date: _____

Skill: Representing and analyzing mathematical situations and structure using algebraic symbols

Unit 2: Algebra: *Assessment 2*

Mark the answer that is represented by the variable.

1. $76.2 \times y = 1,371.6$
   - ○ A. $y = 16$
   - ○ B. $y = 18$
   - ○ C. $y = 21$
   - ○ D. $y = 20$

2. $164.9 \times y = 4,617.2$
   - ○ A. $y = 28$
   - ○ B. $y = 29$
   - ○ C. $y = 31$
   - ○ D. $y = 17$

3. $852.35 \times y = 10,228.2$
   - ○ A. $y = 9$
   - ○ B. $y = 10$
   - ○ C. $y = 11$
   - ○ D. $y = 12$

4. $87.43 \times y = 1,836.03$
   - ○ A. 18
   - ○ B. 20
   - ○ C. 21
   - ○ D. 22

5. $109.9 \times y = 6,154.4$
   - ○ A. 46
   - ○ B. 56
   - ○ C. 58
   - ○ D. 60

6. $6,789.4 \times y = 604,256.6$
   - ○ A. 89
   - ○ B. 91
   - ○ C. 88
   - ○ D. 90

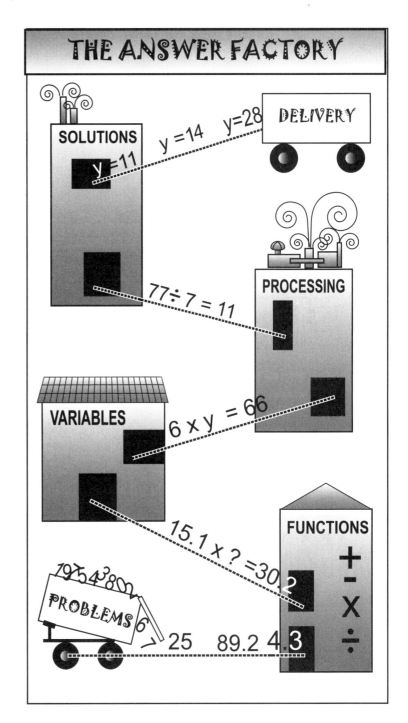

Name: _____ Date: _____

Unit 2: Algebra: *Assessment 2 (cont.)*

Solve each equation. Mark the answer that is represented by the variable.

7. $8m + 18 = 90$
- A. 8
- B. 9
- C. 12
- D. 6

9. $78y - 98 = 1{,}384$
- A. 12
- B. 15
- C. 17
- D. 19

8. $12y - 161 = 127$
- A. 20
- B. 18
- C. 24
- D. 26

10. $876y - 17{,}115 = 19{,}677$
- A. 32
- B. 41
- C. 42
- D. 44

Look at the table. Then answer each question.

Rule: $y = 0.74z + 2.10$	
y	**z**
	5.8
	12

11. What is the value of *y* when the value of *z* is 5.8?
- A. 6.932
- B. 6.392
- C. 63.92
- D. 639.2

12. What is the value of *y* when the value of *z* is 12?
- A. 10.98
- B. 10.21
- C. 10.89
- D. 109.8

Name: _____ Date: _____

Skill: Analyzing the characteristics and properties of two- and three-dimensional geometric shapes, and developing mathematical arguments about geometric relationships

Unit 3: Geometry: *Practice Activity 1*

Just a Tip: A **polygon** is a two-dimensional closed figure made up of line segments. The line segments cannot cross.

Name each polygon. If the figure is not a polygon, write one sentence that explains why it is not a polygon.

Example: *Answer:* The figure is a quadrilateral.

1. _____

2. _____

Use your protractor to measure each angle. Then define the angle in three ways. The first one is done for you.

3.   *Answer:* ∠GST, 45°, acute   4. _____

5. _____   6. _____

7. _____   8. _____

9. ![angle ABC] _____

WAKE-UP WORD PROBLEM: Louise spends between $95.00 and $150.00 each week at the grocery store. What is the least amount of money Louise could spend during a five-week period?

_____

What is the greatest amount of money Louise could spend during a five-week period?

_____

Name: _____ Date: _____

Skill: Analyze characteristics and properties of two and three-dimensional geometric shapes, and develop mathematical arguments about geometric relationships

Unit 3: Geometry: *Practice Activity 2*

Just a Tip: Intersecting lines meet or cross each other. **Parallel lines** never intersect. **Perpendicular lines** intersect to form right angles.

Identify each of the following types of lines as either intersecting, parallel, or perpendicular. The first one is completed as an example.

1.    *parallel lines* _____

2. 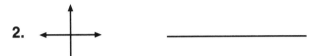 _____

3.  _____

4. 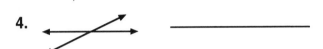 _____

5. Draw an example of parallel lines.

6. Draw an example of perpendicular lines.

Just a Tip: Adjacent angles have a common vertex and a common side but no interior points that are the same. **Complementary angles** are two angles whose measurements total 90 degrees. **Supplementary angles** are two angles whose measurements total 180 degrees.

Use your protractor. Identify each pair of angles as adjacent angles, complementary angles, or supplementary angles.

7.  _____

8.  _____

9. _____

10.  _____

Name: _____ Date: _____

Unit 3: Geometry: *Practice Activity 2 (cont.)*

Identify each triangle as a **scalene triangle**, **isosceles triangle**, **equilateral triangle**, **acute triangle**, **right triangle**, or **obtuse triangle**. More than one term may apply to each triangle.

11. _____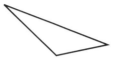

12. _____

13. _____

14. _____

Identify each quadrilateral as a **parallelogram**, **rhombus**, **rectangle**, **square**, **trapezoid**, or **kite**.

15. _____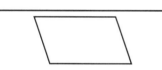

18. _____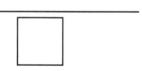

16. _____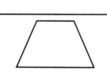

19. _____

17. _____

20. _____

Extension Activities: Direct students to create pictures using intersecting, parallel, and perpendicular lines. Have them identify each type of line in their drawings.

Have students look for and record sightings of various types of triangles and various types of quadrilaterals that they see in their everyday lives.

Name: _____ Date: _____

Skill: Analyzing the characteristics and properties of two- and three-dimensional geometric shapes, and developing mathematical arguments about geometric relationships

Unit 3: Geometry: *Practice Activity 3*

Perimeter   **P = sum of the lengths of all sides**

6.7 in.

6.7 in

     Example: The perimeter of the kite is 26.80 inches.

Find the perimeter of each figure.

1. _____

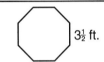
$3\frac{1}{2}$ ft.

2. _____

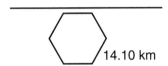
14.10 km

Volume   **V = l(length of base) x w(width of base) x h(height of prism)**

     Example: The volume of the cube is 216 cubic inches.

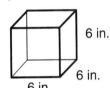
6 in.

6 in.

6 in.

Find the volume of each shape.

3. _____

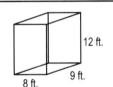
12 ft.

9 ft.

8 ft.

4. _____

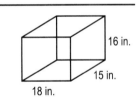
16 in.

15 in.

18 in.

Area   **A = l(length) x w(width)**   **Area of triangle = $\frac{1}{2}$b(base) x h(height)**

    Example: The area of the square is 49 square inches.

7 in.

Find the area of each shape.

5. _____

4 ft.

7 ft.

6. _____

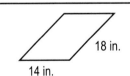
18 in.

14 in.

7. _____

3 in.

1 1/2 in.

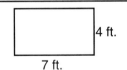
26 1/2 ft.

WAKE-UP WORD PROBLEM: Jamal is ordering fence materials for his rectangular backyard. How much fencing material should he order?

_____

24 1/2 ft.

Name: _____ Date: _____

Skill: Analyzing characteristics and properties of two- and three-dimensional geometric shapes, and developing mathematical arguments about geometric relationships

Unit 3: Geometry: *Assessment 1*

Read each problem carefully. Then mark the best answer.

1. Which of the following represents a set of parallel lines?

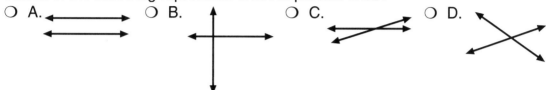

2. Which of the following represents an equilateral triangle?

3. Which of the following represents a scalene triangle?

4. Which of the following represents complementary angles?

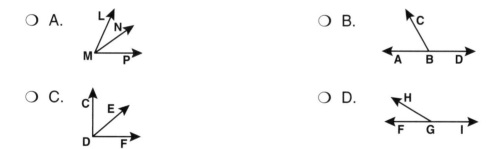

5. Which of the following represents supplementary angles?

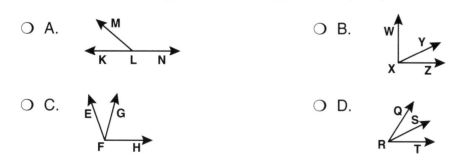

Name: _____ Date: _____

Unit 3: Geometry: *Assessment 1 (cont.)*

6. Find the perimeter of the irregular shape.

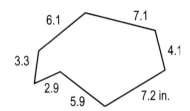

- ○ A. 36.7 inches
- ○ B. 36.6 inches
- ○ C. 37.2 inches
- ○ D. 39.6 inches

7. Which of the following is NOT a polygon?

 ○ A.   ○ B.   ○ C.   ○ D.

8. What is the volume of the rectangular prism?

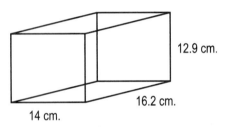

- ○ A. 2955.72 cubic centimeters
- ○ B. 2925.72 cubic centimeters
- ○ C. 29.25 cubic centimeters
- ○ D. 292.572 cubic centimeters

Use your protractor to solve questions 9–10.

9. What is the measurement of ∠CDE?
- ○ A. 60 degrees
- ○ B. 65 degrees
- ○ C. 75 degrees
- ○ D. 90 degrees

10. What is the measurement of ∠EFG?
- ○ A. 90 degrees
- ○ B. 100 degrees
- ○ C. 115 degrees
- ○ D. 120 degrees

Name: _____ Date: _____

Skill: Specifying locations and describing spatial relationships using coordinate geometry and other representational systems

Unit 3: Geometry: *Practice Activity 4*

Name the point for each ordered pair. The first number represents the *x*-axis, and the second number represents the *y*-axis.

1. (3,1) _____

2. (9,1) _____

3. (6,4) _____

4. (10,5) _____

5. (7,2) _____

6. (5,5) _____

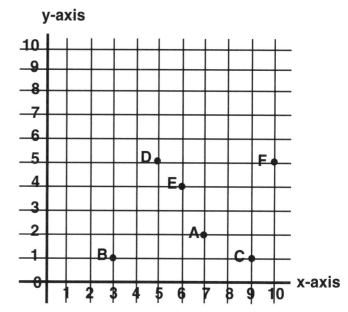

Give the coordinates of each point. Coordinates are written in an ordered pair (*x, y*).

7. V _____

8. W _____

9. Y _____

10. X _____

11. Z _____

12. U _____

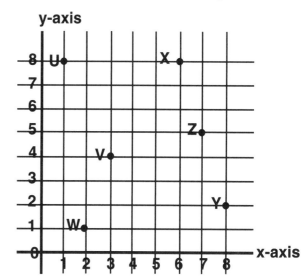

37

Name: _____ Date: _____

Skill: Specifying locations and describing spatial relationships using coordinate geometry and other representational systems

Unit 3: Geometry: *Practice Activity 5*

Complete the table for the function represented by each equation. Then graph the function as a line on the graph.

1.
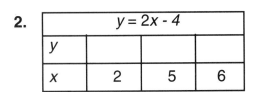

$y = 3x$			
y			
x	2	3	4

2.
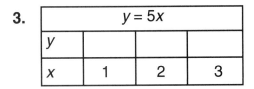

$y = 2x - 4$			
y			
x	2	5	6

3.
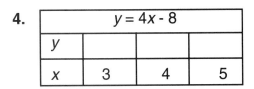

$y = 5x$			
y			
x	1	2	3

4.
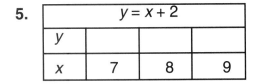

$y = 4x - 8$			
y			
x	3	4	5

5.

$y = x + 2$			
y			
x	7	8	9

WAKE-UP WORD PROBLEM: Nancy works as a lifeguard at her neighborhood pool and earns $7.25 an hour. She works 17 hours the first week of May, 20 hours during the second week of May, 22 hours during the third week of May, and 19 hours during the fourth week of May. How much money does Nancy earn when lifeguarding during these four weeks?

_____

Name: _____ Date: _____

Skill: Specifying locations and describing spatial relationships using coordinate geometry and other representational systems

Unit 3: Geometry: *Assessment 2*

1. What are the coordinates of the point E?
   - ○ A. (4,9)
   - ○ B. (10,12)
   - ○ C. (12,6)
   - ○ D. (5,7)

2. What are the coordinates of the point D?
   - ○ A. (5,9)
   - ○ B. (5,8)
   - ○ C. (7,5)
   - ○ D. (9,5)

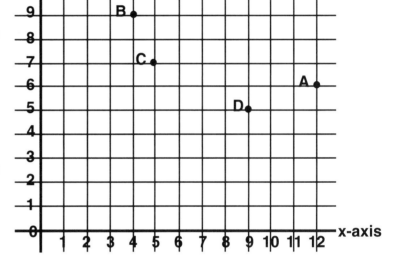

3. What are the coordinates of the point C?
   - ○ A. (7,7)
   - ○ B. (7,5)
   - ○ C. (5,7)
   - ○ D. (7,9)

4. What are the coordinates of the point B?
   - ○ A. (4,9)
   - ○ B. (9,4)
   - ○ C. (5,9)
   - ○ D. (4,10)

5. What are the coordinates of the point A?
   - ○ A. (6,12)
   - ○ B. (10,8)
   - ○ C. (12,6)
   - ○ D. (12,8)

Name: _____   Date: _____

Unit 3: Geometry: *Assessment 2 (cont.)*

6. What is the point for the ordered pair (8,5)?
    ○ A. I
    ○ B. G
    ○ C. J
    ○ D. K

7. What is the point for the ordered pair (7,5)?
    ○ A. I
    ○ B. H
    ○ C. J
    ○ D. K

8. What is the point for the ordered pair (9,10)?
    ○ A. J
    ○ B. G
    ○ C. H
    ○ D. I

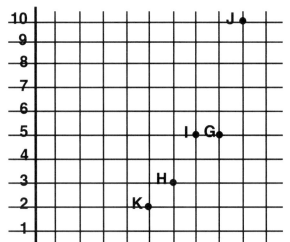

9. What is the point for the ordered pair (6,3)?
    ○ A. I
    ○ B. J
    ○ C. H
    ○ D. K

10. What is the point for the ordered pair (5,2)?
    ○ A. G
    ○ B. H
    ○ C. K
    ○ D. J

Name: _____ Date: _____

Unit 3: Geometry: *Assessment 2 (cont.)*

Complete the table for the function represented by each equation.

c = 10d				
c	#11 _____	#12 _____	#13 _____	#14 _____
d	3	6	7	9

11. On the table, c is equivalent to _____ for #11.
    ○ A. 30
    ○ B. 20
    ○ C. 25
    ○ D. 40

12. On the table, c is equivalent to _____ for #12.
    ○ A. 50
    ○ B. 60
    ○ C. 40
    ○ D. 70

13. On the table, c is equivalent to _____ for #13.
    ○ A. 35
    ○ B. 80
    ○ C. 60
    ○ D. 70

14. On the table, c is equivalent to _____ for #14.
    ○ A. 90
    ○ B. 80
    ○ C. 70
    ○ D. 60

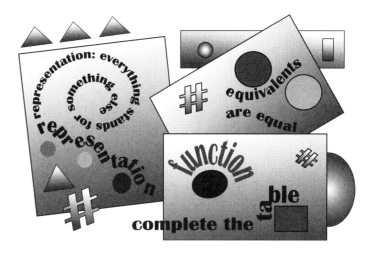

Name: _____ Date: _____

Review of Four Previously Taught NCTM Standards

- **Understanding patterns, relations, and functions**

- **Representing and analyzing mathematical situations and structures using algebraic symbols.**

- **Analyzing the characteristics and properties of two- and three-dimensional geometric shapes, and developing mathematical arguments about geometric relationships**

- **Specifying locations and describing spatial relationships using coordinate geometry**

1. What is the point for the ordered pair (5,6)?
   - ○ A. A
   - ○ B. F
   - ○ C. H
   - ○ D. C

2. What is the point for the ordered pair (7,3)?
   - ○ A. K
   - ○ B. F
   - ○ C. A
   - ○ D. M

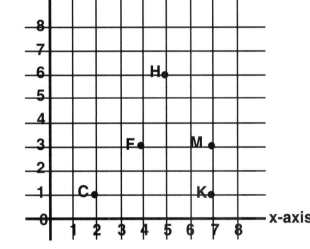

Evaluate each expression.

3. $98.75 \times y = 1382.5$
   - ○ A. $y = 10$
   - ○ B. $y = 12$
   - ○ C. $y = 14$
   - ○ D. $y = 16$

4. $9,876 \times y = 24,690$
   - ○ A. $y = 2.70$
   - ○ B. $y = 2.46$
   - ○ C. $y = 2.5$
   - ○ D. $y = 3.3$

5. Find the volume for the rectangular prism.

   - ○ A. 9.472 cubic centimeters
   - ○ B. 95.721 cubic centimeters
   - ○ C. 94.227 cubic centimeters
   - ○ D. 94.772 cubic centimeters

7.6 cm

2.9   4.3

Name: _____ Date: _____

Review of Four Previously Taught NCTM Standards (cont.)

6. Find the volume for the cube.
   - ○ A. 5,088.448 cubic inches
   - ○ B. 221.88 cubic inches
   - ○ C. 588.48 cubic inches
   - ○ D. 6,948.08 cubic inches

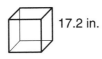

17.2 in.

7. Find the perimeter for the irregular figure.
   - ○ A. 17.8 feet
   - ○ B. 20.1 feet
   - ○ C. 21.0 feet
   - ○ D. 20.07 feet

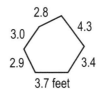

2.8
4.3
3.0
2.9
3.4
3.7 feet

8. Complete the table below for the function represented by the equation.
   - ○ A. 12
   - ○ B. 6
   - ○ C. 9
   - ○ D. 4

$y = 3x - 9$			
x	3	6	7
y	0		12

9. Complete the pattern.

   17, _____, 272, 1,088, 4,352, 17,408
   - ○ A. 78
   - ○ B. 68
   - ○ C. 72
   - ○ D. 174

10. Which angle represents an obtuse angle?

   ○ A.

   ○ B.

   ○ C.

   ○ D.

Name: _____ Date: _____

Skill: Applying transformations and using symmetry to analyze mathematical situations

Unit 3: Geometry: *Practice Activity 6*

Just a Tip: Transformations change the position of figures. Three types of transformations are a translation, a rotation, and a reflection.

Choose the answer that best describes the movement between figure A and figure B.

Example: A  B

   ○ A. translation
   ○ B. rotation
   ● C. reflection
   ○ D. none of the above

1. ○ A. translation
   ○ B. rotation
   ○ C. reflection
   ○ D. none of the above

   A  B

2. ○ A. translation
   ○ B. rotation
   ○ C. reflection
   ○ D. none of the above

   A  B

3. ○ A. translation
   ○ B. rotation
   ○ C. reflection
   ○ D. none of the above

   A   B

4. ○ A. translation
   ○ B. rotation
   ○ C. reflection
   ○ D. none of the above

   A   B

5. ○ A. translation
   ○ B. rotation
   ○ C. reflection
   ○ D. none of the above

   A B

Name: _____ Date: _____

Unit 3: Geometry: *Practice Activity 6 (cont.)*

6. ○ A. translation
○ B. rotation
○ C. reflection
○ D. none of the above

A B

7. ○ A. translation
○ B. rotation
○ C. reflection
○ D. none of the above

A 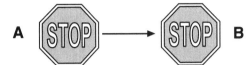 B

8. ○ A. translation
○ B. rotation
○ C. reflection
○ D. none of the above

A  B

9. ○ A. translation
○ B. rotation
○ C. reflection
○ D. none of the above

A  B

10. ○ A. translation
○ B. rotation
○ C. reflection
○ D. none of the above

A  B

Name: _____ Date: _____

Skill: Applying transformations and using symmetry to analyze mathematical situations

Unit 3: Geometry: *Practice Activity 7*

Example: "A" should be marked
Choose the answer for the object that has a line of symmetry.

● A.   ○ B.   ○ C.

1. Choose the answer for the object that has a line of symmetry.

○ A.   ○ B.   ○ C.

2. Choose the answer for the object that has a line of symmetry.

○ A.   ○ B.   ○ C.

3. Choose the answer for the object that has a line of symmetry.

○ A.   ○ B.   ○ C.

4. Choose the answer for the object that has a line of symmetry.

○ A.   ○ B.   ○ C.

5. Choose the answer for the object that has a line of symmetry.

○ A.   ○ B.    ○ C.

6. Choose the answer for the object that has a line of symmetry.

○ A.   ○ B.   ○ C.

Name: _____ Date: _____

Unit 3: Geometry: *Practice Activity 7 (cont.)*

7. How many lines of symmetry does the figure have?

- ○ A. 0
- ○ B. 1
- ○ C. 2
- ○ D. 3

8. How many lines of symmetry does the figure have?

- ○ A. 0
- ○ B. 2
- ○ C. 4
- ○ D. 6

9. How many lines of symmetry does the figure have?

- ○ A. 0
- ○ B. 1
- ○ C. 2
- ○ D. 4

10. Which figure is congruent to the figure in the box?

- ○ A.
- ○ B.
- ○ C.
- ○ D.

11. Which figure is congruent to the figure in the box?

- ○ A.
- ○ B.
- ○ C.
- ○ D.

WAKE-UP WORD PROBLEM: Jesse spends five days skiing with some friends. Every day during his trip, he spends a total of $3.25 on breakfast, $4.75 on lunch, and $7.50 on dinner. How much money does Jesse spend on breakfast, lunch, and dinner during all five days?

Name: _____   Date: _____

Skill: Applying transformations and using symmetry to analyze mathematical situations

Unit 3: Geometry: *Assessment 3*

Choose the answer that best describes the movement between figure A and figure B.

1. ○ A. translation
    ○ B. rotation
    ○ C. reflection
    ○ D. none of the above

2. ○ A. translation
    ○ B. rotation
    ○ C. reflection
    ○ D. none of the above

3. ○ A. translation
    ○ B. rotation
    ○ C. reflection
    ○ D. none of the above

4. ○ A. translation
    ○ B. rotation
    ○ C. reflection
    ○ D. none of the above

5. ○ A. translation
    ○ B. rotation
    ○ C. reflection
    ○ D. none of the above

6. Which object has a line of symmetry?

    ○ A.   ○ B.

    ○ C.   ○ D.

Name: _____ Date: _____

Unit 3: Geometry: *Assessment 3 (cont.)*

7. Which object does NOT have a line of symmetry?

    ○ A.   ○ B.    ○ C.    ○ D.

8. Which object does NOT have a line of symmetry?

    ○ A.   ○ B.   ○ C.   ○ D.

9. How many lines of symmetry does the figure have?
    ○ A. 4
    ○ B. 6
    ○ C. 8
    ○ D. 12

10. How many lines of symmetry does the figure have?
    ○ A. 0
    ○ B. 2
    ○ C. 3
    ○ D. 4

11. Which object is congruent to the figure in the box?

  ○ A.   ○ B.   ○ C.   ○ D.

12. Which figure is congruent to the figure in the box?

  ○ A.   ○ B.

        ○ C.   ○ D.

Name: _____ Date: _____

Skill: Using visualization, spatial reasoning, and geometric modeling to solve problems

Unit 3: Geometry: *Practice Activity 8*

Just a Tip: A **two-dimensional shape** is a flat shape, or a figure on a plane.

A **three-dimensional shape** can be defined as a space figure.

Write the measure of the missing angle in each triangle. Hint: The total of the angles in a triangle is always 180°.

1.

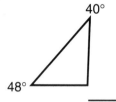

2.

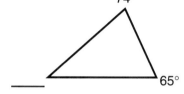

3. Draw a triangle in the box with the following angles: 43°, 66°, 71°.

4. Draw a triangle in the box with the following angles: 64°, 55°, 61°.

Write the measure of the missing angle in each quadrilateral. Hint: The total of the angles in a quadrilateral is always 360°.

5.

6.

7. Draw a quadrilateral in the box with the following angles: 141°, 63°, 89°, 67°.

8. Draw a quadrilateral in the box with the following angles: 125°, 151°, 50°, 34°.

Name: _____ Date: _____

Skill: Using visualization, spatial reasoning, and geometric modeling to solve problems

Unit 3: Geometry: *Practice Activity 9*

Identify each of the following shapes.

Example: Look at the net. The net could be cut and folded to make a _____.

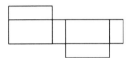

Answer: Rectangular prism

1. Look at the net. The net could be cut and folded to make a _____.

2. Look at the net. The net could be cut and folded to make a _____.

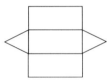

3. Look at the net. The net could be cut and folded to make a _____.

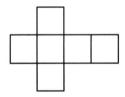

Identify each shape. Then write the number of faces, edges, and vertices each shape has.

Example: Cube   6 faces, 12 edges, 8 vertices

4.   shape: _____

_____ faces   _____ edges   _____ vertices

5.   shape: _____

_____ faces   _____ edges   _____ vertices

6.   shape: _____

_____ faces   _____ edges   _____ vertices

Name: _____ Date: _____

Skill: Use visualization, spatial reasoning, and geometric modeling to solve problems

Unit 3: Geometry: *Practice Activity 10*

Just a Tip: Transformations change the position of figures. Three types of transformations are a **translation**, a **rotation**, and a **reflection**.

Follow the directions given.

Example: Look at the trapezoid in the box. Draw a reflection of the trapezoid in the space provided.

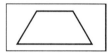

1. Look at the octagon in the box. Draw a translation of the octagon in the space provided.

2. Look at the triangle in the box. Draw a 90-degree rotation of the triangle in the space provided.

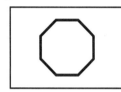

3. Look at the balloon in the box. Draw a 45-degree rotation of the balloon in the space provided.

4. Look at the square in the box. Draw a 180-degree rotation of the square in the space provided.

Extension Activity: Provide and/or have students select several favorite pictures of objects from magazines. Have students draw the object and then draw a translation, reflection, and/or rotation of each object.

Name: _____ Date: _____

Skill: Using visualization, spatial reasoning, and geometric modeling to solve problems

Unit 3: Geometry: *Practice Activity 11*

Just a Tip: The **surface area** is the total area of all the faces of a three-dimensional figure. The formula for finding surface area for a prism is **SA = ph + 2B**. Multiply the perimeter (**p**) of the base figure times the height (**h**) of the prism. Then multiply the area of the base (**B**) times two. Finally, add those two numbers together.

The **volume** is the amount of space a three-dimensional figure encloses. Find the volume of a cube or prism by multiplying the length times the width times the height.

Find the surface area for each rectangular prism.

Example: 3 in. 1 in. 2 in.

Answer: The surface area is 22 square inches.

1. _____

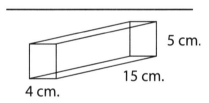 5 cm. 15 cm. 4 cm.

2. _____

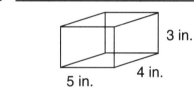 3 in. 5 in. 4 in.

Find the volume for each shape.

3. _____

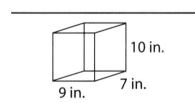 10 in. 9 in. 7 in.

4. _____

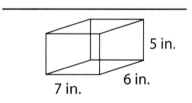 5 in. 7 in. 6 in.

5. _____

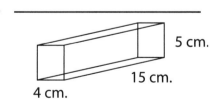 5 cm. 15 cm. 4 cm.

6. _____

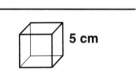 **5 cm**

7. _____

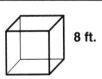 **8 ft.**

8. _____

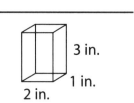 3 in. 1 in. 2 in.

Name: _____ Date: _____

Skill: Using visualization, spatial reasoning, and geometric modeling to solve problems

Unit 3: Geometry: *Assessment 4*

Choose the answer that best describes the movement of the object.

1. ○ A. the picture shows a translation of the lamp
   ○ B. the picture shows a reflection of the lamp
   ○ C. the picture shows a 95-degree rotation of the lamp
   ○ D. the picture shows a 125-degree rotation of the lamp

2. Which net could be cut and folded to show a rectangular prism?

   ○ A. 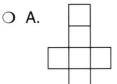　○ B. 　○ C. 　○ D.

3. What is the volume of the rectangular prism?
   ○ A. 118 cubic inches
   ○ B. 108 cubic inches
   ○ C. 112 cubic inches
   ○ D. 106 cubic inches

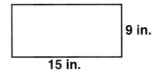

   9 in.
   4 in.
   3 in.

4. What is the area of the rectangle?
   ○ A. 125 square inches
   ○ B. 185 square inches
   ○ C. 135 square inches
   ○ D. 115 square inches

   9 in.
   15 in.

5. Which picture shows a 45-degree rotation of the octagon on the grid?

   　○ A. 　○ B. 　○ C. 　○ D.

6. What is the volume of the rectangular prism?
   ○ A. 17.86 cubic centimeters
   ○ B. 17.68 cubic centimeters
   ○ C. 201.63 cubic centimeters
   ○ D. 206.12 cubic centimeters

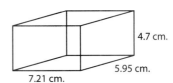

   4.7 cm.
   5.95 cm.
   7.21 cm.

Name: _____   Date: _____

Unit 3: Geometry: *Assessment 4 (cont.)*

7. What is the area of the rectangle?
    ○ A. 218 square feet
    ○ B. 204 square feet
    ○ C. 208.8 square feet
    ○ D. 212 square feet

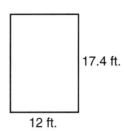

17.4 ft.

12 ft.

8. What is the measurement of the missing angle?
    ○ A. 236 degrees
    ○ B. 56 degrees
    ○ C. 58 degrees
    ○ D. 65 degrees

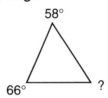

58°

66°   ?

9. What is the measurement of the missing angle?
    ○ A. 68 degrees
    ○ B. 71 degrees
    ○ C. 72 degrees
    ○ D. 74 degrees

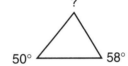

?

50°   58°

10. What is the measurement of the missing angle?
    ○ A. 71 degrees
    ○ B. 81 degrees
    ○ C. 84 degrees
    ○ D. 79 degrees

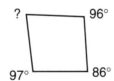

?   96°

97°   86°

11. Find the surface area of the rectangular prism.
    ○ A. 16 square inches
    ○ B. 30 square inches
    ○ C. 40 square inches
    ○ D. 22 square inches

4 in.

2 in.

2 in.

12. Find the surface area of the rectangular prism.
    ○ A. 142 square feet
    ○ B. 60 square feet
    ○ C. 195 square feet
    ○ D. 56 square feet

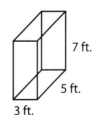

7 ft.

5 ft.

3 ft.

Name: _____ Date: _____

Skill: Understanding the measurable attributes of objects and the units, systems, and processes of measurement

Unit 4: Measurement: *Practice Activity 1*

Convert each unit of measurement.

Customary length, capacity, and weight *Example:* 7 cups = 56 ounces

1. 144 ounces = _____ pounds

2. 40 quarts = _____ gallons

3. 12,000 pounds = _____ tons

4. 12 pints = _____ cups

5. 21 cups = _____ ounces

6. 32 yards = _____ feet

7. 15 quarts = _____ cups

8. 5 quarts = _____ pints

9. 30 gallons = _____ quarts

10. 45 pounds = _____ ounces

> 12 inches = 1 foot
> 3 feet = 1 yard
> 5,280 feet = 1 mile
> 16 ounces = 1 pound
> 2,000 pounds = 1 ton
> 8 ounces = 1 cup
> 2 cups = 1 pint
> 2 pints = 1 quart
> 4 quarts = 1 gallon

Metric length, capacity, and mass

11. 5,000 meters = _____ kilometers

12. 800 centimeters = _____ meters

13. 50 millimeters = _____ centimeters

14. 9 centimeters = _____ millimeters

15. 7 metric tons = _____ kilograms

16. 12 grams = _____ milligrams

17. 5,000 kilograms = _____ metric tons

18. 10,000 meters = _____ kilometers

19. 25 centimeters = _____ millimeters

20. 5,000 milligrams = _____ grams

> 10 milimeters = 1 centimeter
> 100 centimeters = 1 meter
> 1,000 meters = 1 kilometer
> 1,000 milligrams = 1 gram
> 1,000 grams = 1 kilogram
> 1,000 kilograms = 1 metric ton

WAKE-UP WORD PROBLEM: Joanne makes two quarts of lemonade for her party. How many pints of lemonade does this equal? _____

Extension Activity: Give each student a copy of a recipe and/or have him/her bring one from home. Ask the students to convert the recipe from one unit to another within the same system.

56

Name: _____ Date: _____

Skill: Understanding measurable attributes of objects and the units, systems, and processes of measurement

Unit 4: Measurement: *Practice Activity 2*

Just a Tip: Area is the number of square units needed to cover a figure or specific space. Find the area by multiplying length times width.

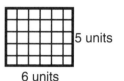

5 units

6 units

Area = 30 square units

Perimeter is the distance around a closed figure. Find the perimeter by adding the lengths of all sides of a figure.

4 cm

4 cm

Perimeter = 16 cm

Find the area of each shape described below.

1. A rectangle with length = 4.12 feet, width = 7.95 feet _____

2. A rectangle with length = 6 inches, width = 12 inches _____

3. A rectangle with length = 21 inches, width = 29.2 inches _____

4. A square with a length and width of 14.7 feet _____

5. A square with a length and width of 9 centimeters _____

Find the perimeter of each figure.

6. _____

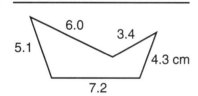

6.0

3.4

5.1

4.3 cm

7.2

7. _____

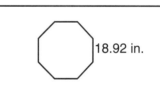

18.92 in.

8. _____

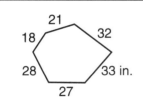

21

18

32

28

33 in.

27

9. _____

13.62   13.95

15.75   14.78 in.

14.42

10. _____

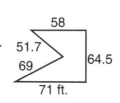

58

51.7

69

64.5

71 ft.

Name: _____ Date: _____

Skill: Understanding the measurable attributes of objects and the units, systems, and processes of measurement

Unit 4: Measurement: *Practice Activity 3*

Using reference materials, such as an almanac, encyclopedia, or the Internet, find a chart that shows the conversion factors for changing measurements from metric to standard and from standard to metric.

Make conversions between systems.

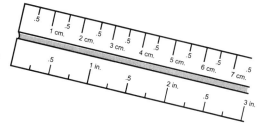

> **Example:** How many centimeters are in 12 inches?
>
> *Answer:* There are 30 centimeters in 12 inches.

1. How many meters are in 8 yards? _____

2. How many kilometers are in 3 miles? _____

3. How many centimeters are in 9 inches? _____

4. How many feet are in 5 meters? _____

5. How many miles are in 4 kilometers? _____

6. How many liters are in 7 liquid quarts? _____

7. How many quarts are in 8 liquid liters? _____

8. How many inches are in 6 meters? _____

Convert the temperatures below from one measurement system to another.

To convert from Fahrenheit to Celsius, subtract 32 from the temperature and multiply by 5/9.

To convert from Celsius to Fahrenheit, multiply the temperature by 9/5 and add 32.

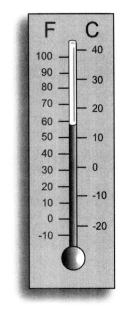

9. $30°C =$ _____ $° F$

10. $21°C =$ _____ $° F$

11. $78°F =$ _____ $° C$

12. $32°F =$ _____ $° C$

Name: _____ Date: _____

Skill: Understanding the measurable attributes of objects and the units, systems, and processes of measurement

Unit 4: Measurement: *Assessment 1*

1. How many cups are in 64 fluid ounces?
   - ○ A. 6
   - ○ B. 8
   - ○ C. 10
   - ○ D. 12

2. How many meters are in 15 kilometers?
   - ○ A. 1,500
   - ○ B. 15,000
   - ○ C. 18,000
   - ○ D. 500

3. How many centimeters are in 100 millimeters?
   - ○ A. 10
   - ○ B. 12
   - ○ C. 6
   - ○ D. 9

4. About how many miles are in 12 kilometers?
   - ○ A. 7.5
   - ○ B. 5
   - ○ C. 21
   - ○ D. 18.2

5. About how many liters are in 6 liquid quarts?
   - ○ A. 5
   - ○ B. 6.3
   - ○ C. 5.7
   - ○ D. 7.2

6. How many gallons are in 48 quarts?
   - ○ A. 6
   - ○ B. 8
   - ○ C. 10
   - ○ D. 12

Name: _____ Date: _____

Skill: Applying appropriate techniques, tools, and formulas to determine measurements

Unit 4: Measurement: *Practice Activity 4*

Just a Tip: The angles in a triangle always total 180°.

Look at each right triangle. Determine the measurement of the missing angle.

Example: *Answer:* The missing angle is 50°.

1. 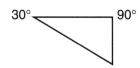   **2.** 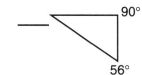   **3.**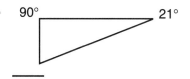

Look at each acute triangle. Determine the measurement of the missing angle.

4.   **5.**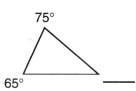

6.    **7.**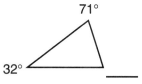

Look at each obtuse triangle. Determine the measurement of the missing angle.

8. 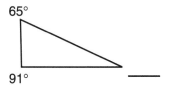   **9.**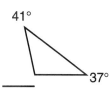

10.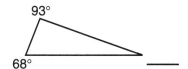

Name: _____ Date: _____

Skill: Applying appropriate techniques, tools, and formulas to determine measurements

Unit 4: Measurement: *Practice Activity 5*

Just a Tip: The formula for finding the area of a circle is **A = π x r x r.**
Remember, π = 3.14.

Find the **area** of each circle.

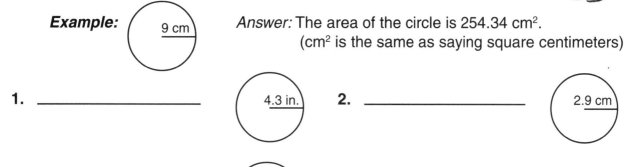

Example: 9 cm

Answer: The area of the circle is 254.34 cm².
(cm² is the same as saying square centimeters)

1. _____ 4.3 in.   2. _____ 2.9 cm

3. _____ 5 cm

Just a Tip: The **area** of a shape is the number of square units that cover it. To find the area of a rectangle, use the formula, **A = l(length) x w(width).** To find the area of a parallelogram, use the formula, **A = b(base) x h(height).**

Find the area of each rectangle or parallelogram.

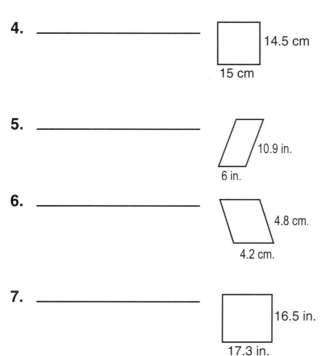

4. _____   14.5 cm
   15 cm

5. _____   10.9 in.
   6 in.

6. _____   4.8 cm.
   4.2 cm.

7. _____   16.5 in.
   17.3 in.

Name: _____ Date: _____

Unit 4: Measurement: *Practice Activity 5 (cont.)*

Just a Tip: To find the area of a triangle, you can look at a parallelogram that has the same base and height as the triangle. The area of a triangle, is $\frac{1}{2}$ the area of a parallelogram with the same base and height. So, **$A = \frac{1}{2}bh$**.

Find the area of each triangle.

8. _____

12 in.

9 in.

9. _____

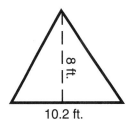

8 ft.

10.2 ft.

10. _____

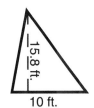

15.8 ft.

10 ft.

11. _____

12.3 cm

9.75 cm

WAKE-UP WORD PROBLEM: Gracie records the amount of money she spends for five months on groceries. She spends $27.55, $36.95, $45.12, $33.75, and $28.99. What was the average amount of money that Gracie spent on groceries?

_____

Extension Activity: Have students draw several circles. Then ask them to determine the circumference of each circle.

Name: _____ Date: _____

Skill: Applying appropriate techniques, tools, and formulas to determine measurements

Unit 4: Measurement: *Practice Activity 6*

Circumference of a circle

Just a Tip: Find the circumference of a circle by using the formula $C = 2\pi r$. Remember, $\pi = 3.14$.

Find the circumference of each circle.

Example: *Answer:* The circumference of the circle is 16.96 inches.

1. _____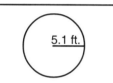
5.1 ft.

2. _____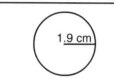
1.9 cm

3. _____
3.3 m

4. _____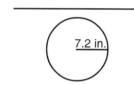
7.2 in.

5. _____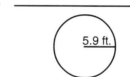
5.9 ft.

6. _____
0.2 m

7. _____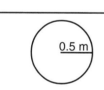
0.5 m

8. _____
0.7 m

9. _____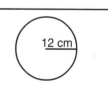
12 cm

Find the radius of a circle with the given circumference.

10. Circumference = 121 inches _____

11. Circumference = 18 feet _____

12. Circumference = 25.6 inches _____

WAKE-UP WORD PROBLEM: Ming and her sister, Kimiko, are collecting money for the school fundraiser. Ming collects $181.78. Kimiko collects half as much money as Ming. How much money is Kimiko able to collect for the school fundraiser?

Name: _____ Date: _____

Skill: Applying appropriate techniques, tools, and formulas to determine measurements

Unit 4: Measurement: *Assessment 2*

1. What is the circumference of the circle?
   - A. 6.28 meters
   - B. 6.51 meters
   - C. 6.15 meters
   - D. 17.4 meters

2. What is the circumference of the circle?
   - A. 190.9 inches
   - B. 109.9 inches
   - C. 19.9 inches
   - D. 199.09 inches

3. If the radius of a circle is 4.5 inches, what is the circumference of the circle?
   - A. 26.28 inches
   - B. 28.26 inches
   - C. 282.6 inches
   - D. 29.68 inches

4. If the circumference of a circle is 95 centimeters, what is the radius of the circle?
   - A. 15.13 centimeters
   - B. 15.71 centimeters
   - C. 21.78 centimeters
   - D. 157.18 centimeters

5. What is the area of the circle?
   - A. 803.84 square feet
   - B. 296.06 square feet
   - C. 201.06 square feet
   - D. 198.96 square feet

6. What is the area of the circle?
   - A. 60.07 square inches
   - B. 59.62 square inches
   - C. 58.08 square inches
   - D. 43.80 square inches

Name: _____ Date: _____

Unit 4: Measurement: *Assessment 2 (cont.)*

7. What is the formula for finding the area of a parallelogram?
   ○ A. $A = 2\pi r$
   ○ B. $A = lw$
   ○ C. $A = bh$
   ○ D. $A = b - h$

8. What is the area of the rectangle?
   ○ A. 71.58 square inches
   ○ B. 178.2 square inches
   ○ C. 78.64 square inches
   ○ D. 70.69 square inches

7.25 in.

9.75 in.

9. What is the area of the parallelogram?
   ○ A. 258.91 square centimeters
   ○ B. 259.61 square centimeters
   ○ C. 209.85 square centimeters
   ○ D. 213.78 square centimeters

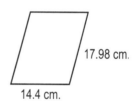

17.98 cm.

14.4 cm.

10. What is the area of the rectangle?
   ○ A. 57.22 square feet
   ○ B. 572.25 square feet
   ○ C. 578.25 square feet
   ○ D. 278.5 square feet

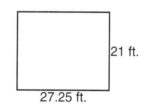

21 ft.

27.25 ft.

11. What is the area of the triangle?
   ○ A. 51.02 square inches
   ○ B. 48.18 square inches
   ○ C. 49.14 square inches
   ○ D. 38 square inches

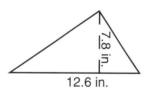

7.8 in.

12.6 in.

12. What is the area of the triangle?
   ○ A. 252 square feet
   ○ B. 258 square feet
   ○ C. 25.2 square feet
   ○ D. 216 square feet

28 ft.

18 ft.

Name: _____ Date: _____

Review of Four Previously Taught NCTM Standards

- **Applying transformations and using symmetry to analyze mathematical situations**

- **Using visualization, spatial reasoning, and geometric modeling to solve problems**

- **Understanding the measurable attributes of objects and the units, systems, and pro-cesses of measurement**

- **Applying appropriate techniques, tools, and formulas to determine measurements**

1. Look at Figure A. Then look at Figure B. Figure B is a _____ of Figure A.
    - ○ A. rotation
    - ○ B. translation
    - ○ C. reflection
    - ○ D. none of the above

    A   B

2. What is the circumference of the circle?
    - ○ A. 71 inches
    - ○ B. 1557.40 inches
    - ○ C. 155.74 inches
    - ○ D. 157 inches

    24.8 in.

3. Which object has a line of symmetry?

    ○ A.   ○ B.   ○ C.   ○ D.

4. What is the area of the triangle?
    - ○ A. 200.09 square inches
    - ○ B. 2,000.09 square inches
    - ○ C. 20.1 square inches
    - ○ D. 400.18 square inches

    21.4 in.
    18.7 in.

5. Find the measure of the unknown angle.
    - ○ A. 72°
    - ○ B. 75°
    - ○ C. 81°
    - ○ D. 118°

    68°
    ?   40°

Name: _____ Date: _____

Review of Four Previously Taught NCTM Standards

6. Find the measure of the missing angle.
- ○ A. 68°
- ○ B. 69°
- ○ C. 71°
- ○ D. 75°

7. Which picture shows a net for a cylinder?

○ A. 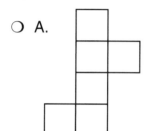 ○ B. 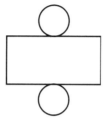 ○ C. 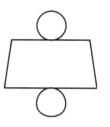 ○ D.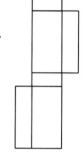

8. What is the perimeter of the irregular figure?
- ○ A. 9.2 inches
- ○ B. 9.8 inches
- ○ C. 11.5 inches
- ○ D. 11.7 inches

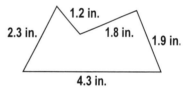

9. What is the volume of the rectangular prism?
- ○ A. 312.48 cubic centimeters
- ○ B. 217.62 cubic centimeters
- ○ C. 2,643.09 cubic centimeters
- ○ D. 2,437.34 cubic centimeters

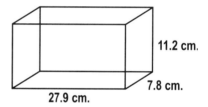

10. How many ounces are in 15 pounds?
- ○ A. 214
- ○ B. 240
- ○ C. 204
- ○ D. 24

Name: _____ Date: _____

Skill: Formulating questions that can be addressed with data and collecting, organizing, and displaying relevant data to answer them

Unit 5: Data Analysis and Probability: *Practice Activity 1*

Read the histogram. Then answer the questions below.

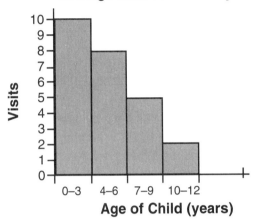

Average Number of Yearly Doctor Visits

Example: According to the histogram, which age group visited the doctor most frequently?
Answer: Children between 0–3 visited the doctor most often.

1. According to the histogram, which age group visited the doctor least frequently?

   _____

2. According to the histogram, how many more times would an average 2-year-old visit a doctor than an average 11-year-old during a year-long period? _____

3. According to the histogram, how many fewer times would an average 8-year-old visit the doctor than an average 5-year-old during a year-long period? _____

Read the line graph. Then answer the questions below.

4. How much cooler is the average September day than the average July day?

   _____

5. How much warmer is the average July day than the average May day? _____

6. Which month, on average, has the coolest temperature? _____

7. Based on the information provided in the line graph, what would the average temperature for June, July, and August be? _____

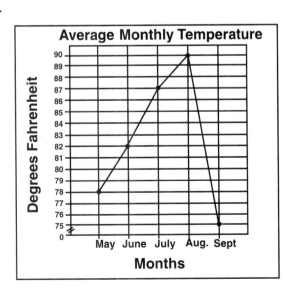

Name: _____ Date: _____

Skill: Formulating questions that can be addressed with data and collecting, organizing, and displaying relevant data to answer them

Unit 5: Data Analysis and Probability: *Practice Activity 2*

Read the table. Then answer questions 1–3.

Example: How many more bottles of water were sold at the tennis match than at the basketball game?

Answer: Three hundred seventy-five more bottles of water were sold at the tennis match.

NUMBER OF BOTTLES OF WATER SOLD AT SIX SPORTING EVENTS
Tennis
Baseball
Basketball
Football
Ice Skating
Soccer

= 250 Bottles

1. How many more bottles of water were sold at the football and basketball events than at the ice skating and soccer events? _____

2. If each bottle of water is sold for $0.95, how much money was made on all the bottles of water sold at the ice-skating event? _____

3. What was the average number of bottles of water sold at all six sporting events?

_____

Extension Activity: Have students select something they are interested in finding out about their classmates. Then ask students to take a survey and record their information. Have them make both a bar graph and a pictograph displaying the information they uncovered. Students can share their findings with their classmates.

Name: _____ Date: _____

Unit 5: Data Analysis and Probability: *Practice Activity 2 (cont.)*

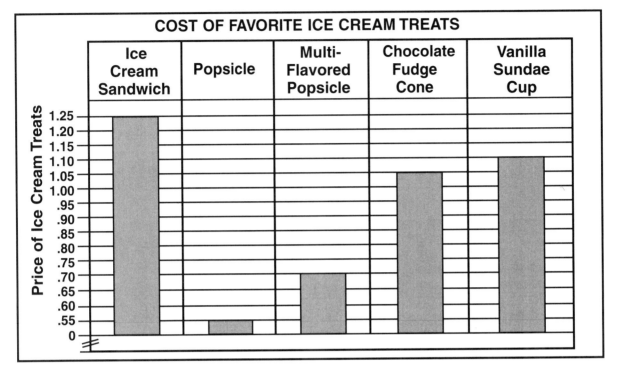

COST OF FAVORITE ICE CREAM TREATS

(Bar graph — Price of Ice Cream Treats)

Ice Cream Sandwich	Popsicle	Multi-Flavored Popsicle	Chocolate Fudge Cone	Vanilla Sundae Cup
1.25	.55	.70	1.05	1.10

4. How much would it cost to purchase eight popsicles? _____

5. How much more would it cost to purchase a chocolate fudge cone and a vanilla sundae cup than it would cost to purchase an ice cream sandwich and a popsicle? _____

6. Ms. James wants to reward her class for a job well done. She purchases fifteen ice cream sandwiches and nine multi-flavored popsicles to reward her students. How much money does Ms. James spend in all? _____

7. You have $3.00, and you buy three treats. Which three treats could you afford to buy?

_____

8. Make a table in the space provided below that displays the same information as in the bar graph.

Name: _____ Date: _____

Skill: Formulating questions that can be addressed with data and collecting, organizing, and displaying relevant data to answer them

Unit 5: Data Analysis and Probability: *Assessment 1*

Read the histogram. Then answer questions 1–2.

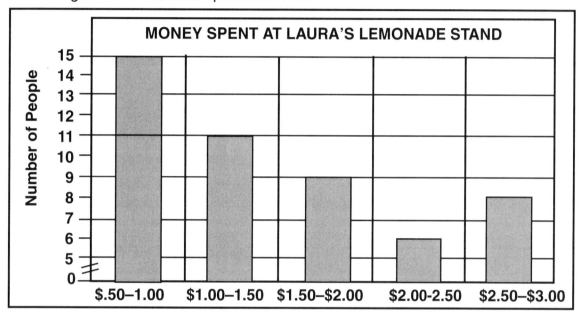

1. How many more people spent between $1.00–$1.50 than between $2.50–$3.00 at Laura's Lemonade Stand?
   - ○ A. 9
   - ○ B. 12
   - ○ C. 3
   - ○ D. 8

2. How many of the people that visited Laura's Lemonade Stand spent $2.00 or less?
   - ○ A. 27
   - ○ B. 35
   - ○ C. 37
   - ○ D. 102

Read the table. Then answer questions 3–5.

Monday in June	# of Passengers
1st	3,004
2nd	2,098
3rd	4,566
4th	2,345
5th	2,321

3. How many passengers rode the bus on the first and second Monday of the month?
   - ○ A. 5,102
   - ○ B. 5,112
   - ○ C. 5,015
   - ○ D. 4,068

4. How many total passengers rode the bus on the first, third, and fifth Mondays of June?
   - ○ A. 9,871
   - ○ B. 9,801
   - ○ C. 8,791
   - ○ D. 9,891

5. Make an assumption, based on the information in the table.
   - ○ A. Fewer people ride the bus at the end of the month.
   - ○ B. More people ride the bus at the end of the month.
   - ○ C. People do not like to ride the bus.

Name: _____ Date: _____

Unit 5: Data Analysis and Probability: *Assessment 1 (cont.)*

Read the line graph. Then answer questions 6–10.

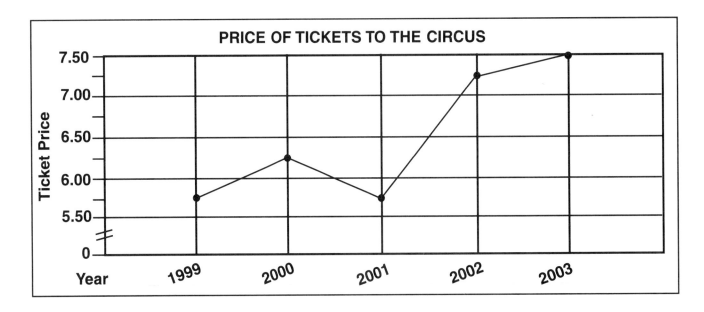

6. How much more would it cost a family of four to go to the circus in 2002 than it cost a family of four to go to the circus in 1999?
   - ○ A. $6.00
   - ○ B. $12.00
   - ○ C. $8.00
   - ○ D. $7.25

7. During which two years was the price of tickets the same?
   - ○ A. 1999 and 2002
   - ○ B. 1999 and 2001
   - ○ C. 2002 and 2003
   - ○ D. 2000 and 2001

8. What was the average ticket price for the years listed in the graph?
   - ○ A. $7.00
   - ○ B. $5.75
   - ○ C. $6.75
   - ○ D. $6.50

9. José buys fifty tickets to the circus for his company in 2002 and 2003. How much more does José spend on circus tickets in 2003?
   - ○ A. $15.00
   - ○ B. $12.50
   - ○ C. $8.75
   - ○ D. $10.00

10. Make an assumption, based on the information provided on the line graph.
    - ○ A. The cost of tickets has increased $0.25 every year.
    - ○ B. The largest increase in expenses for the circus must have occurred between 2001 and 2002.
    - ○ C. The cost of tickets is decreasing every year.
    - ○ D. The cost of a ticket in 2004 will definitely be higher than in 2003.

Name: _____ Date: _____

Skill: Selecting and using appropriate statistical methods to analyze data

Unit 5: Data Analysis and Probability: *Practice Activity 3*

Just a Tip: When you are looking for the **median**, you are looking for the middle number in a group of numbers arranged in numerical order. For example, if you are looking for the median of the numbers {3, 6, 4, 3, 1, 7, 9}, first, you have to put the numbers in numerical order {1, 3, 3, 4, 6, 7, 9}. Then, determine the number that is in the middle of all the numbers after they have been put in numerical order. So, the median for the set of numbers given would be 4. If there are two numbers in the middle of the set, find the average of those two numbers.

When you are looking for the **mode**, you are looking for the number or numbers that appear most frequently in a set of data. So, if you are looking for the mode for the set of numbers {3, 5, 4, 2, 1, 7, 1, 5, 4, 5}, the mode would be 5, since it appears the most number of times (there are three 5s in the set of data).

When you are looking for the **range**, you are looking for the difference between the greatest and the least numbers in a group of numbers, so you'll need to subtract. For example, to find the range of the numbers {3, 5, 7, 1, 8, 2, 2, 4}, you would need to find the difference between the largest number (8) and the smallest number (1). Since 8 - 1 = 7, the range of the data is 7.

When you are looking for the **mean**, you are looking for the average. The easiest way to find the average is to add up all the numbers you are averaging and then divide by how many numbers you are averaging. For example, if you are looking for the mean of the numbers {4, 6, 3, 7}, first, add up all four numbers (20). Then, divide 20 by how many numbers you are averaging (4); so, 20 ÷ 4 = 5.

When you are looking for the **outlier**, it is the number that is so different from the rest of the data that it is best to leave it out. Leaving out the outlier may change the mean, median, mode, and range. For example, in the set of numbers {60, 62, 64, 66, 238, 68}, the outlier is 238.

Find the **range** for each set of data below.

1. 32, 21, 45, 52   _____

2. 101, 112, 112, 117, 121, 124   _____

3. 300, 401, 368, 417, 322, 188   _____

4. 74, 68, 72, 71, 80, 97, 95   _____

Find the **mode** for each set of data below.

5. 51, 52, 57, 51, 65, 87   _____

6. 112, 121, 117, 115, 141, 117, 118   _____

7. 207, 264, 301, 301, 312, 301, 312, 117   _____

8. 188, 219, 119, 221, 401, 206, 119   _____

Name: _____ Date: _____

Unit 5: Data Analysis and Probability: *Practice Activity 3 (cont.)*

Find the **median** for each set of data below.

9. 17, 6, 18, 21, 27, 26, 18, 17 _____

10. 12, 11, 10, 4, 6, 9, 15, 25 _____

11. 101, 111, 112, 117, 121, 125, 137 _____

Find the **mean** for each set of data below.

12. 45, 49, 56, 61, 75, 82 _____

13. 171, 121, 156, 145, 131 _____

14. 201, 210, 215, 221, 225, 201 _____

Find the **outlier** for each set of data below.

15. 101, 121, 117, 115, 112, 308 _____

16. 15, 18, 21, 16, 14, 35, 12 _____

17. 200, 201, 212, 251, 501, 221 _____

18. 14, 15, 16, 15, 17, 18, 81, 20, 21 _____

WAKE-UP WORD PROBLEM: Samantha sleeps 10 hours Monday night, 6 hours Tuesday night, 8 hours Wednesday and Thursday night, 9 hours Friday night, and 7 hours Saturday night. What is the average amount of sleep Samantha gets during all six nights?

_____

Name: _____ Date: _____

Skill: Selecting and using appropriate statistical methods to analyze data

Unit 5: Data Analysis and Probability: *Practice Activity 4*

Find the mean, median, mode, and range for each set of data.

	Mean	Median	Mode	Range
1. 45, 47, 39, 42, 41, 52, 56, 52				
2. 2, 12, 9, 4, 4, 8, 7, 6, 5, 11				
3. 101, 121, 171, 156, 145, 137				
4. 211, 215, 221, 225, 236, 238, 241				
5. 19, 20, 27, 32, 36, 41, 47				

Extension Activity: In the space below, write down five test grades from your most recent math tests. Then find the mean, median, mode, and range of this data.

Scores: _____ _____ _____ _____ _____

Mean: _____

Median: _____

Mode: _____

Range: _____

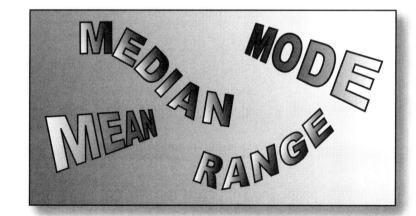

Name: _____　　Date: _____

Skill: Selecting and using appropriate statistical methods to analyze data

Unit 5: Data Analysis and Probability: *Practice Activity 5*

Stem and Leaf Plots

Follow the steps and organize the information on the table in a **stem and leaf plot**.

Time Spent Reading During the Weekend	
Student #	**Time (in minutes)**
1	25
2	55
3	115
4	135
5	150
6	65
7	68
8	115

First, order the data from least to greatest in rows. There should be a separate row for each tens digit.

Then, make two columns. Separate the ones digits, or leaves, from the other digits, or stems.

　　　　　　　　Stem　　　　Leaves

Add a key: 11 | 5 = 115 minutes

　　　　　76

Name: _____   Date: _____

Skill: Selecting and using appropriate statistical methods to analyze data

Unit 5: Data Analysis and Probability: *Assessment 2*

Look at each set of data. Then answer the question.

1. Find the range of the set of data: 145, 137, 165, 117, 174, 206, 119, 118, 119
    - ○ A. 79
    - ○ B. 84
    - ○ C. 95
    - ○ D. 89

2. Find the mean of the set of data: 121, 165, 117, 174, 181, 187, 119
    - ○ A. 165
    - ○ B. 161
    - ○ C. 156
    - ○ D. 152

3. Find the mean of the set of data: 217, 354, 186, 386, 395, 341
    - ○ A. 313.2
    - ○ B. 315
    - ○ C. 317.5
    - ○ D. 321

4. Find the mode of the set of data: 141, 145, 129, 137, 145, 146
    - ○ A. 139
    - ○ B. 147
    - ○ C. 140
    - ○ D. 145

5. Find the outlier for the set of data: 75, 86, 81, 79, 75, 211, 76, 84
    - ○ A. 86
    - ○ B. 75
    - ○ C. 211
    - ○ D. 84

6. Find the range of the set of data: 24, 28, 35, 37, 49, 51, 54
    - ○ A. 31
    - ○ B. 27
    - ○ C. 35
    - ○ D. 30

Name: _____ Date: _____

Unit 5: Data Analysis and Probability: *Assessment 2 (cont.)*

7. Genevieve wants to find the average of her test scores for biology. What Genevieve is looking for is called the _____.
   ○ A. mean
   ○ B. mode
   ○ C. range
   ○ D. median

8. Look at the information of the table. Which stem and leaf plot represents the data?

Time Spent Exercising	
Monday	55 minutes
Tuesday	34 minutes
Wednesday	27 minutes
Thursday	38 minutes
Friday	59 minutes

○ A.   **Time Spent Exercising**
　　　　Stem Leaf
　　　　　2 | 7
　　　　　3 | 8
　　　　　5 | 5 9

　　　　Key: 3 | 4 = 34 minutes

○ B.   **Time Spent Exercising**
　　　　Stem Leaf
　　　　　2 | 7 9
　　　　　3 | 4 8
　　　　　5 | 5 9

　　　　Key: 3 | 4 = 34 minutes

○ C.   **Time Spent Exercising**
　　　　Stem Leaf
　　　　　2 | 7
　　　　　3 | 4 8
　　　　　5 | 5 9

　　　　Key: 3 | 4 = 34 minutes

○ D.   **Time Spent Exercising**
　　　　Stem Leaf
　　　　　2 | 7
　　　　　3 | 4 8
　　　　　5 | 5 9
　　　　　7 | 1

　　　　Key: 3 | 4 = 34 minutes

9. What number represents 27 on the stem and leaf plot?
   ○ A. first number in row for stem #2
   ○ B. second number in row for stem #2
   ○ C. first number in row for stem #3
   ○ D. last number in row for stem #5

10. What number represents 59 on the stem and leaf plot?
    ○ A. first number in row for stem #2
    ○ B. first number in row for stem #5
    ○ C. second number in row for stem #5
    ○ D. second number in row for stem #3

　　　　　　　　78

Name: _____   Date: _____

Skill: Understanding and applying basic concepts of probability

Unit 5: Data Analysis and Probability: *Practice Activity 6*

Ming wanted to find out the favorite subject of her fellow schoolmates. There are five hundred students enrolled at Ming's school. She polled one hundred students and then used her results to predict the number of students who would give each answer if all five hundred students were surveyed.

Read the table. Then answer questions 1–4.

Subject	Students
Science	28
Language Arts	42
Math	21
Social Studies	5
French	4

Example: Based on this information, about how many of the total number of students like science best?

Answer: Based on this information, one hundred forty of the students like science best.

Just a Tip: To figure out each answer, start by changing information from the table into a decimal. For example, 28 students like science best. Since we can predict that this pattern is consistent with the feelings of all five hundred students, you can multiply to find out the number of all students who like science best: 0.28 x 500 = 140. About 140 of the 500 students like science best.

1. Based on this information, about how many of the total number of students like language arts best?

   _____

2. Based on this information, about how many of the total number of students like math best?

   _____

3. Based on this information, about how many of the total number of students like social studies best?

   _____

4. Based on this information, about how many of the total number of students like French best?

   _____

Name: _____ Date: _____

Unit 5: Data Analysis and Probability: *Practice Activity 6 (cont.)*

Read the table. Then answer questions 5–9.

Candidate	# of Votes
Roley	25
Perez	33
Jenkins	17
Bishop	88
Arnold	37

* Two hundred students polled

5. Based on this information, if 1,000 people voted, how many people would vote for Roley?

   _____

6. Based on this information, if 1,000 people voted, how many people would vote for Perez?

   _____

7. Based on this information, if 1,000 people voted, how many people would vote for Jenkins?

   _____

8. Based on this information, if 1,000 people voted, how many people would vote for Bishop?

   _____

9. Based on this information, if 1,000 people voted, how many people would vote for Arnold?

   _____

WAKE-UP WORD PROBLEM: There are seventy-two children at the class picnic. Seventeen of the children are wearing sun hats, and twenty-three of the kids
are wearing baseball hats. Ms. Lloyd calls out the name of a student who forgot to
bring his or her lunch. What is the probability that the student who forgot his or her
lunch is wearing a hat?

Name: _____ Date: _____

Skill: Understanding and applying basic concepts of probability

Unit 5: Data Analysis and Probability: *Practice Activity 7*

Look at the spinner. Then answer questions 1–3.

Example: Write a fraction that represents the probability that the spinner will land on #7.

Answer: There is a $\frac{1}{8}$ chance the spinner will land on #7.

1. Write a ratio that represents the probability that the spinner will land on #4.

_____

2. Write a percent that represents the probability that the spinner will land on #4.

_____

3. Write a decimal that represents the probability that the spinner will land on #1.

_____

Look at the bag of marbles. Then answer questions 4–8.

4. Write a fraction that represents the probability of selecting a green marble.

_____

5. Write a fraction that represents the probability of selecting a yellow marble.

_____

6. Which color(s) are you most likely to select?

_____

7. Write a ratio that shows your chances of selecting a yellow marble.

_____

8. Write a fraction that shows the probability of selecting a red marble.

_____

Extension Activity: Have students look at spinners from several favorite board games. Discuss: Are the spinners fair? Why or why not?

81

Name: _____ Date: _____

Skill: Understanding and applying basic concepts of probability

Unit 5: Data Analysis and Probability: *Assessment 3*

Look at the information in the table. Then answer questions 1–5.

Favorite Sport	# of Students
Soccer	32
Baseball	27
Volleyball	22
Basketball	15
Other	54

*150 students polled from Sanchez Elementary; Total student population at Sanchez Elementary = 600 students

1. Based on the information in this table, if all 600 students at Sanchez Elementary had been polled, how many would have selected soccer as their favorite sport?
   - A. 128
   - B. 118
   - C. 102
   - D. 28

2. Based on the information in this table, if all 600 students at Sanchez Elementary had been polled, how many would have selected baseball as their favorite sport?
   - A. 118
   - B. 108
   - C. 112
   - D. 88

3. Based on the information in this table, if all 600 students at Sanchez Elementary had been polled, how many would have selected volleyball as their favorite sport?
   - A. 181
   - B. 85
   - C. 88
   - D. 108

4. Based on the information in this table, if all 600 students at Sanchez Elementary had been polled, how many would have selected basketball as their favorite sport?
   - A. 65
   - B. 58
   - C. 61
   - D. 60

5. Based on the information in this table, if all 600 students at Sanchez Elementary had been polled, how many would have selected the category "other" as their favorite sport?
   - A. 121
   - B. 108
   - C. 206
   - D. 216

82

Name: _____ Date: _____

Unit 5: Data Analysis and Probability: *Assessment 3*

Look at the spinner.

6. Which ratio represents your chances of spinning a 7 or 4?
- ○ A. 2:6
- ○ B. 2:4
- ○ C. 3:8
- ○ D. 5:10

7. Which fraction represents your chances of spinning a 3 or 9?
- ○ A. $\frac{1}{2}$
- ○ B. $\frac{1}{3}$
- ○ C. $\frac{2}{3}$
- ○ D. $\frac{1}{4}$

8. Which percentage represents your chances of spinning a 6 or 11?
- ○ A. 41%
- ○ B. 38%
- ○ C. 35%
- ○ D. 33%

9. Which fraction represents your chances of spinning an even number?
- ○ A. $\frac{1}{2}$
- ○ B. $\frac{1}{4}$
- ○ C. $\frac{2}{3}$
- ○ D. $\frac{1}{3}$

10. Which percentage represents your chances of spinning an odd number?
- ○ A. 67%
- ○ B. 68%
- ○ C. 72%
- ○ D. 75%

Name: _____ Date: _____

End-of-Book Review

1. Which of the following represents the word form for the number 27,658,429?
   - ○ A. twenty-seven million, six hundred fifty-eight thousand, four hundred twenty-nine
   - ○ B. twenty-seven thousand, six hundred fifty eight thousand, four hundred nine
   - ○ C. twenty-seven hundred thousand, six hundred fifty-eight thousand, four hundred nineteen
   - ○ D. twenty-seven million, six hundred eight thousand, four hundred twenty-nine

2. Solve the problem: 0.96 x 4.71 ÷ 0.2
   - ○ A. 22.608
   - ○ B. 22.651
   - ○ C. 25.06
   - ○ D. 4.523

3. Noelle earns approximately $1,565.00 babysitting during a twelve-month period. Assuming that she earns about the same amount of money each month, how much does she earn each month?
   - ○ A. $135
   - ○ B. $130
   - ○ C. $150
   - ○ D. $210

4. Round this number to the nearest hundred thousand: 286,541.
   - ○ A. 200,000
   - ○ B. 250,000
   - ○ C. 300,000
   - ○ D. 285,000

5. Which percent represents the ratio 24:100?
   - ○ A. 32%
   - ○ B. 26%
   - ○ C. 12%
   - ○ D. 24%

6. Evaluate the expression: $9.24 \times y = 138.6$.
   - ○ A. $y = 15$
   - ○ B. $y = 13$
   - ○ C. $y = 12$
   - ○ D. $y = 9$

Name: _____ Date: _____

End-of-Book Review (cont.)

7. Which sentence is true?
   - ○ A. The lines are perpendicular.
   - ○ B. The lines are parallel.
   - ○ C. The lines intersect.
   - ○ D. The lines are crooked.

8. Find the perimeter of the irregular figure.
   - ○ A. 34.3 inches
   - ○ B. 33.4 inches
   - ○ C. 35.7 inches
   - ○ D. 334 inches

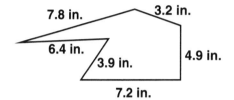

9. Look at figure A. Then look at figure B. Choose the answer that best describes the movement between figure A and figure B.
   - ○ A. rotation
   - ○ B. reflection
   - ○ C. translation
   - ○ D. forestry

10. Find the measure of the unknown angle.
    - ○ A. 14
    - ○ B. 102
    - ○ C. 114
    - ○ D. 104

11. Ellie saves $824.98 over summer vacation. Her brother, Charlie, saves $\frac{1}{2}$ as much money. How much did Charlie save?
    - ○ A. $412.49
    - ○ B. $415.39
    - ○ C. $112.49
    - ○ D. $441.49

12. What is the area of the rectangle?
    - ○ A. 305.7 square centimeters
    - ○ B. 367.5 square centimeters
    - ○ C. 316.7 square centimeters
    - ○ D. 309.7 square centimeters

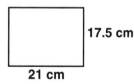

13. Estimate the difference: 92,643 - 37,865 =
    - ○ A. 57,600
    - ○ B. 60,000
    - ○ C. 5,500
    - ○ D. 50,000

Name: _____ Date: _____

End-of-Book Review (cont.)

14. What is the value in bold? 17,468,721
    ○ A. thousands
    ○ B. millions
    ○ C. ten thousands
    ○ D. hundred thousands

15. How many tons are in 24,000 pounds?
    ○ A. 12
    ○ B. 10
    ○ C. 15
    ○ D. 9

16. How many cups are in 12 quarts?
    ○ A. 46
    ○ B. 48
    ○ C. 24
    ○ D. 32

17. The triangle below can best be described as _____.
    ○ A. equilateral
    ○ B. acute
    ○ C. obtuse
    ○ D. right

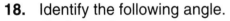

18. Identify the following angle.
    ○ A. acute
    ○ B. straight
    ○ C. obtuse
    ○ D. right

Answer Keys

Unit 1: Practice Activity 1 (Pages 2–3)

1. eighty-seven million, nine hundred eighty-nine thousand, nine; 87,989,009; 80,000,000 + 7,000,000 + 900,000 + 80,000 + 9,000 + 9
2. twelve million, eight hundred ninety-seven thousand, ninety-eight; 12,897,098; 10,000,000 + 2,000,000 + 800,000 + 90,000 + 7,000 + 90 + 8
3. three hundred nine thousand, eight hundred ninety-seven; 309,897; 300,000 + 9,000 + 800 + 90 + 7
4. sixty-seven million, ninety-eight thousand, nine hundred eighty-one; 67,098,981; 60,000,000 + 7,000,000 + 90,000 + 8,000 + 900 + 80 + 1
5. twenty-one million, nine hundred eighty-seven thousand, seven hundred sixty-seven; 21,987,767; 20,000,000 + 1,000,000 + 900,000 + 80,000 + 7,000 + 700 + 60 + 7
6. eight hundred nine thousand, nine hundred eighty-seven; 809,987; 800,000 + 9,000 + 900 + 80 + 7
7. ten million, nine hundred eighty-nine thousand, five hundred forty-three; 10,989,543; 10,000,000 + 900,000 + 80,000 + 9,000 + 500 + 40 + 3
8. sixty-five million, nine hundred eighty-seven thousand, eight hundred seventy-seven; 65,987,877; 60,000,000 + 5,000,000 + 900,000 + 80,000 + 7,000 + 800 + 70 + 7
9. two million, ninety-eight thousand, eight hundred seventy-one; 2,098,871; 2,000,000 + 90,000 + 8,000 + 800 + 70 + 1
10. ninety-eight million, seven hundred eighty-six thousand, one hundred eleven; 98,786,111; 90,000,000 + 8,000,000 + 700,000 + 80,000 + 6,000 + 100 + 10 + 1

Unit 1: Practice Activity 2 (Page 4)

1. 5
2. 90,000,000
3. 5,000,000,000
4. 900,000,000,000
5. 60
6. 300,000,000,000
7. 8
8. 2
9. 5 thousandths or 0.005
10. 10,000,000
11. 90,000
12. 2 hundredths or 0.02
13. 7
14. 1 tenth or 0.01
15. 900,000

WAKE-UP WORD PROBLEM: SIxty students ordered a lunch from the cafeteria.

Unit 1: Practice Activity 3 (Pages 5–6)

1. 75/100 or 3/4; 0.75; 75%; 75:100
2. 55/100 or 11/20; 0.55; 55%; 55:100
3. 1/10; 0.10; 10%; 10:100
4. 17/100; 0.17; 17%; 17:100
5. 12/100; 0.12; 12%; 12:100
6. 21/100; 0.21: 21%; 21:100
7. 65/100 or 13/20; 0.65; 65%; 65:100 or 13:20
8. 81/100; 0.81; 81%; 81:100
9. 100/100 or 1/1; 1.00; 100%; 100:100
10. 25%
11. 17%
12. 75%
13. 84%
14. 2%

WAKE-UP WORD PROBLEM: One hundred seventy-five of the campers signed up for camp are girls.

Unit 1: Practice Activity 4 (Page 7)

1. 0.001
2. 1/4
3. 0.301
4. 5.55
5. 19,878,098; 9,876,098; 9,098,987; 9,008,098
6. 211,098,876; 210,876,098; 210,546,876; 210,098,876
7. 6,987,987; 6,987,098; 6,432,098; 3,546,876
8. 788,654; 788,543; 788,091; 786,876; 708,876
9. 21,987,096; 21,765,908; 21,543,765; 21,098,876
10. 0.0001; 0.001; 0.01; 1.0
11. 0.007; 0.70; 0.78; 0.87
12. 0.0072; 0.06; 0.076; 0.67
13. 0.043; 0.074; 0.34; 0.42
14. 0.0021; 0.0210, 0.210; 2.10

Unit 1: Assessment 1 (Pages 8–9)

1. B
2. B
3. C
4. C
5. A
6. B
7. C
8. D
9. A
10. D
11. C
12. A

13. A
14. B
15. B

Unit 1: Practice Activity 5 (Page 10)
1. 210.9767
2. 0.007296
3. 2.338
4. 5,272,151.5
5. 0.025
6. 1,634,400
7. 6,990,562.5
8. 44,341,200
9. 2,740.5
10. 51,958.67
11. 100,000
12. 11.835
13. 975,917.25
14. 29,830

WAKE-UP WORD PROBLEM: Mark earns $5,097.48 in one year.

Unit 1: Practice Activity (Pages 11–12)
Number sentences may vary. Examples are given.
1. $216.75 - $14.75 = $202; $202 + $78.95 = $280.95; Tom earns $280.95.
2. $289.50 ÷ 10 = $28.95; Sarah Lee collects about $28.95 a day.
3. 182 x 2 = 364; 364 ÷ 2 = 182; The Police Department responds to 182 calls during January.
4. 186 x 24 = 4,464; Denise buys 4,464 hamburger buns in all.
5. $5.00 ÷ 12 = $0.42; $6.99 ÷ 24 = $0.29; $0.42 - $0.29 = $0.13; It will cost Laurel about $0.13 less per bottle to buy bottled water at the discount store.
6. $85.50 x 3 = $256.50; Mr. Craig spends $256.50 on his electric bill in June.
7. $430.00 x 3 = $1,290.00; $1,290.00 x 10% = $129.00; He saves $129.00.
8. 60 x 24 = 1,440; 1,440 x 365 = 525,600; There are 525,600 minutes in a year.
9. 514 - 212 = 302; 302 + 216 = 518; Mario has 518 marbles in his collection.

Unit 1: Practice Activity 7 (Page 13)
1. 2 x -6
2. -3 x 5
3. -2 x (4 x -3)
4. (2 x 3) x -2
5. -5
6. -6
7. 0
8. 0

9. (-2 x 3) + (-2 x -4)
10. (-3 x 5) + (-3 x 6)
11. (-4 x 2) - (-4 x 5)
12. (-6 x 3) - (-6 x 6)
13. -18
14. 20
15. 12

WAKE-UP WORD PROBLEM: The temperature is 73°F degrees by the following Friday.

Unit 1: Assessment 2 (Pages 14–15)
1. B
2. D
3. C
4. C
5. D
6. C
7. B
8. C
9. B
10. A
11. C
12. A

Unit 1: Practice Activity 8 (Page 16)
1. 16,000
2. 14,000
3. 43,000
4. 56,000
5. 188,000
6. 115,000
7. 18,000
8. 87,000
9. 54,000
10. 24,000
11. 19,000
12. 641,000

WAKE-UP WORD PROBLEM: About 1,700 people attended the concert on Friday and Saturday night.

Unit 1: Practice Activity 9 (Page 17)
1. 1,200,000
2. 1,000,000
3. 400,000
4. 2,300,000
5. 2,000,000
6. 8,000,000
7. 12,000,000
8. 9,000,000
9. 1,000,000
10. 2,000,000
11. $34.20
12. $234.40

13. $12.30
14. $45.80
15. $35.40
16. $122.89
17. $1,232.99
18. $676.51
19. $432.44
20. $1,088.36

Unit 1: Practice Activity 10 (Pages 18–19)
1. They work about 50 hours a week.
2. About 1,340,000 live in both places altogether.
3. She spends about $190.00 altogether.
4. Wilson will spend about $40,000 more.
5. Maggie earns about $100.
6. They have about $1.90 altogether.
7. She can save about $20 buying the game at the first website.

Unit 1: Assessment 3 (Pages 20–21)
1. B
2. D
3. D
4. A
5. A
6. B
7. C
8. B
9. B
10. C
11. A
12. D

Review of Three Previously Taught NCTM Standards (Pages 22–23)
1. A
2. C
3. C
4. D
5. A
6. D
7. D
8. C
9. C
10. A
11. C
12. B

Unit 2: Practice Activity 1 (Page 24)
1. 81, 729
2. 464, 232
3. 833, 849
4. 2,448, 7,344

5. $4.90
6. $5.85
7. $7.75
8. $3.00 + (5 x 0.95) = $7.75
9. 4 pounds
WAKE-UP WORD PROBLEM: She will have to pay $101.02 in all.

Unit 2: Practice Activity 2 (Page 25)
1. 17 inches
2. 29 inches
3. 15 inches
4. 21.78; 47.92; 231.9
5. 25,344; 101,376; 405,504
6. 2,001; 1,994; 1,987
7. ***
   ***
   ***
8. 12
9. Answers will vary.

Unit 2: Assessment 1 (Page 26)
1. 27,200; 136,000; 544,000
2. 12,527; 12,518; 12,500
3. 257; 128.50; 32.125
4. 567
5. 753; 724
6. $5.75
7. $8.75
8. $13.25
9. 9 pounds
10. Answers will vary. $5.00 + (pounds x $0.75) = total

Unit 2: Practice Activity 3 (Page 27)
1. 4
2. 27
3. 8
4. 52
5. 3
6. 17
7. 9
8. 35
9. 18
10. 95
11. 7
12. 11
13. 30
14. 156
15. 25

Unit 2: Practice Activity 4 (Page 28)
1. 2
2. 48
3. 35
4. 6
5. 4
6. 8
7. 8
8. 11
9. 15
10. 13
11. $y = 9.39$
12. $y = 16.70$
13. $x = 4.2$
14. $y = 20.57$
15. $y = 23.15$
WAKE-UP WORD PROBLEM: It will cost her $422.50 to rent the tables and chairs.

Unit 2: Assessment 2 (Pages 29–30)
1. B
2. A
3. D
4. C
5. B
6. A
7. B
8. C
9. D
10. C
11. B
12. A

Unit 3: Pracrtice Activity 1 (Page 31)
1. No, a circle is made up of curves.
2. The figure is an octagon.
3. ∠GST, 45 degrees, acute
4. ∠MNO, 95 degrees, obtuse
5. ∠TU, 180 degrees, obtuse
6. ∠NOP, 90 degrees, right
7. ∠STU, 25 degrees, acute
8. ∠XYZ, 15 degrees, acute
9. ∠ABC, 120 degrees, obtuse
WAKE-UP WORD PROBLEM: The least amount she could spend is $475. The greatest amount she could spend is $750.

Unit 3: Practice Activity 2 (Pages 32–33)
1. parallel lines
2. perpendicular lines
3. parallel lines
4. intersecting lines
5. teacher check
6. teacher check

7. supplementary
8. complementary
9. adjacent
10. complementary
11. obtuse & scalene triangle
12. right triangle
13. acute & isosceles triangle
14. equilateral & acute
15. parallelogram
16. trapezoid
17. kite
18. square
19. rhombus
20. rectangle

Unit 3: Practice Activity 3 (Page 34)
1. 28 feet
2. 84.6 kilometers
3. 864 cubic feet
4. 4,320 cubic feet
5. 28 square feet
6. 252 square inches
7. 42.25 square inches
WAKE-UP WORD PROBLEM: Jamal needs to order 102 feet of fencing material.

Unit 3: Assessment (Pages 35–36)
1. A
2. C
3. A
4. C
5. A
6. B
7. A
8. B
9. B
10. D

Unit 3: Practice Activity 4 (Page 37)
1. B
2. C
3. E
4. F
5. A
6. D
7. (3,4)
8. (2,1)
9. (8,2)
10. (6,8)
11. (7,5)
12. (1,8)

Unit 3: Practice Activity 5 (Page 38)

1. 6, 9, 12
2. 0, 6, 8
3. 5, 10, 15
4. 4, 8, 12
5. 9, 10, 11

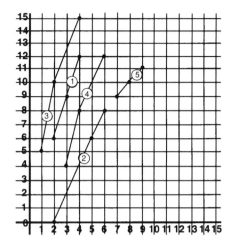

7. A
8. C
9. B
10. D

Unit 3: Practice Activity 7 (Pages 46–47)

1. B
2. B
3. C
4. A
5. C
6. B
7. A
8. C
9. C
10. B
11. C

WAKE-UP WORD PROBLEM: Nancy earns $565.50 lifeguarding during these four weeks.

WAKE-UP WORD PROBLEM: Jesse spends a total of $77.50.

Unit 3: Assessment 2 (Pages 39–41)

1. B
2. D
3. C
4. A
5. C
6. B
7. A
8. A
9. C
10. C
11. A
12. B
13. D
14. A

Unit 3: Assessment 3 (Pages 48–49)

1. A
2. C
3. D
4. A
5. B
6. C
7. C
8. B
9. C
10. A
11. D
12. A

Review of Four Previously Taught NCTM Standards (Pages 42–43)

1. C
2. D
3. C
4. C
5. D
6. A
7. B
8. C
9. B
10. D

Unit 3: Practice Activity 8 (Page 50)

1. 92°
2. 41°
3. The triangle should have the following angles: 43°, 66°, 71°.
3. The triangle should have the following angles: 64°, 55°, 61°.
4. 101°
5. 113°
6. The quadrilateral should have the following angles: 141°, 63°, 89°, 67°.
7. The quadrilateral should have the following angles: 125°, 151°, 50°, 34°.

Unit 3: Practice Activity 6 (Pages 44–45)

1. B
2. D
3. A
4. C
5. D
6. B

Unit 3: Practice Activity 9 (Page 51)

1. cylinder
2. triangular prism
3. cube
4. rectangular prism = 6 faces, 12 edges, 8 vertices

5. square pyramid = 5 faces, 8 edges, 5 vertices
6. triangular prism = 5 faces, 9 edges, 6 vertices

Unit 3: Practice Activity 10 (Page 52)
Teacher check. Students should have followed directions provided.

Unit 3: Practice Activity 11 (Page 53)
1. 310 square centimeters
2. 94 square inches
3. 630 cubic inches
4. 210 cubic inches
5. 300 cubic centimeters
6. 125 cubic centimeters
7. 512 cubic feet
8. 6 cubic inches

Unit 3: Assessment 4 (Pages 54–55)
1. C
2. B
3. B
4. C
5. A
6. C
7. C
8. B
9. C
10. B
11. C
12. A

Unit 4: Practice Activity 1 (Page 56)
1. 9
2. 10
3. 6
4. 24
5. 168
6. 96
7. 60
8. 10
9. 120
10. 720
11. 5
12. 8
13. 5
14. 90
15. 7,000
16. 12,000
17. 5
18. 10
19. 250
20. 5
WAKE-UP WORD PROBLEM: Two quarts of lemonade equals four pints.

Unit 4: Practice Activity 2 (Page 57)
1. 32.75 square feet
2. 72 square inches
3. 613.2 square inches
4. 216.09 square feet
5. 81 square centimeters
6. 26 centimeters
7. 151.36 inches
8. 159 inches
9. 72.52 inches
10. 314.2 feet

Unit 4: Practice Activity 3 (Page 58)
1. 7.3
2. 4.8
3. 22.9
4. 16.4
5. 2.5
6. 6.6
7. 8.5
8. 236.2
9. 86
10. 70
11. 26
12. 0

Unit 4: Assessment 1 (Page 59)
1. B
2. B
3. A
4. A
5. C
6. D

Unit 4: Practice Activity 4 (Page 60)
1. 60 degrees
2. 34 degrees
3. 69 degrees
4. 50 degrees
5. 40 degrees
6. 6 degrees
7. 77 degrees
8. 24 degrees
9. 102 degrees
10. 19 degrees

Unit 4: Practice Activity 5 (Page 61)
1. 58.06 in.^{2}
2. 26.41 in.^{2}
3. 78.5 cm^2
4. 217.5 cm^2
5. 65.4 in.^{2}
6. 20.16 cm^2
7. 285.45 in.^{2}

8. 54 in.²
9. 40.8 ft.²
10. 79 ft.²
11. 59.96 cm²
WAKE-UP WORD PROBLEM: Gracie spent an average of $34.48 on groceries.

Unit 4: Practice Activity 6 (Page 63)
1. 32.03 ft.
2. 11.93 cm
3. 20.72 m
4. 45.22 in.
5. 37.05 ft.
6. 1.26 m
7. 3.14 m
8. 4.40 m
9. 75.36 cm
10. 19.27 in.
11. 2.87 ft.
12. 4.08 in.
WAKE-UP WORD PROBLEM: Kimiko is able to collect $90.89 for the school fundraiser.

Unit 4: Assessment 2 (Pages 64–65)
1. C
2. B
3. B
4. A
5. C
6. C
7. B
8. D
9. A
10. B
11. C
12. A

Review of Four Previously Taught NCTM Standards (Page 66–67)
1. B
2. C
3. C
4. A
5. A
6. B
7. B
8. C
9. D
10. B

Unit 5: Practice Activity 1 (Page 68)
1. 10–12-year-olds
2. 8 more times
3. 3 fewer times
4. 12 degrees cooler
5. 9 degrees warmer
6. September
7. 86 degrees

Unit 5: Practice Activity 2 (Pages 69–70)
1. 3,000 more bottles of water
2. $831.25
3. 2,375
4. $4.40
5. $0.35
6. $25.05
7. Answers will vary.
8. Students will create a table.

Unit 5: Assessment 1 (Pages 71–72)
1. C
2. B
3. A
4. D
5. A
6. A
7. B
8. D
9. B
10. B

Unit 5: Practice Activity 3 (Pages 73–74)
1. 31
2. 23
3. 229
4. 29
5. 51
6. 117
7. 301
8. 119
9. 18
10. 10.5
11. 117
12. 61.3
13. 144.8
14. 212.2
15. 308
16. 35
17. 501
18. 81
WAKE-UP WORD PROBLEM: Samantha sleeps an average of 8 hours each night.

Unit 5: Practice Activity 4 (Page 75)

1. mean = 46.75; median = 46; mode = 52; range = 17
2. mean = 6.8; median = 6.5; mode = 4; range = 10;
3. mean = 138.5; median = 141; mode = no mode; range = 70
4. mean = 226.7; median = 225; mode = no mode; range = 30
5. mean = 31.7; median = 32; mode = no mode; range = 28

Unit 5: Practice Activity 5 (Page 76)

Stem	Leaf
2	5
5	5
6	5 8
11	5 5
13	5
15	0

Unit 5: Assessment 2 (Pages 77–78)

1. D
2. D
3. A
4. D
5. C
6. D
7. A
8. C
9. A
10. C

Unit 5: Practice Activity 6 (Pages 79–80)

1. 210
2. 105
3. 25
4. 20
5. 125
6. 165
7. 85
8. 440
9. 185

WAKE-UP WORD PROBLEM: There is a 40/72 or 5/9 probability that the student is wearing a hat.

Unit 5: Practice Activity 7 (Page 81)

1. 1:8
2. 12.5%
3. 0.125
4. 1/5
5. 1/10
6. purple or red
7. 1:10
8. 3/10

Unit 5: Assessment 3 (Pages 82–83)

1. A
2. B
3. C
4. D
5. D
6. A
7. B
8. D
9. D
10. A

End-of-Book Review (Pages 84–86)

1. A
2. A
3. B
4. C
5. D
6. A
7. B
8. B
9. C
10. D
11. A
12. B
13. D
14. D
15. A
16. B
17. C
18. D

94